SINLESS MIRRORS

PAUL ZEPPELIN

SINLESS MIRRORS

iUniverse books may be ordered through booksellers or by contacting:

iUniverse
1663 Liberty Drive
Bloomington, IN 47403
www.iuniverse.com
844-349-9409

ISBN: 978-1-6632-5003-2 (sc)
ISBN: 978-1-6632-5004-9 (e)

Print information available on the last page.

iUniverse rev. date: 01/19/2023

Contents

Foreword

Paul Zeppelin writes his poetry as a passionate but convincing stream of bright ideas, intense emotions, and laconic clarity without any taboos, whatsoever. He comfortably writes about "Forbidden issues" as religions, sex, politics, and ethics. His verses unearth the deepest layers of our beliefs and doubts, of our dreams and hopes. There is an ancient proverb: "Only the mirrors are sinless."

Paul tried to be a "cold-blooded" mirror reflecting the world we dwell in, but quickly realized that his vibrant curiosity led him into a "no-way-out" labyrinth of, at times, dark conclusions about humans as such.

Being a pragmatic optimist, he often sees a ray of light at the end of his lifelong journey.

Judith Parrish Broadbent
Author of *Golden Days: Stories and Poems of the Central South and Beyond*

P.S. I am eager to mention that Paul never hides his admiration of Irish and Russian limericks, lullabies and counting rhymes.

Prologue

I see my verses as a current of fresh, often unique ideas,
Tightly intertwined with our sincere and ageless emotions.
I hope you like to read them and cross the creek with care.

Final Flight

I don't have all I love,
But I intensely love
All that I have;
A little more the feisty half.

At last, I am a self-indulging hermit,
I am a solo master of my final chapters;
Life was indeed a prearranged disaster,
And I have been a target in that strife…

I am finally and ceaselessly determent
Not to obey the stop or any other sign,
But win the race and cross the finish line,
Then weep at the enigmatic happy end.

I want more distance from the sun,
It only blinds me every day;
I want to be much closer to the moon,
To her caressing silver light;
Please, wait, I do my best, I run,
Please, wait, I am on my way,
I'll see you very, very soon,
I am climbing the stairway's final flight.

My Window

Aloneness
Doesn't enjoy the rite of springs,
Aloneness
Is dispassionate and awfully quiet,
Aloneness
Comes when my cellphone is silent,
But the out-of-date alarm clock rings.

And yet, I offer my poetic craft
To those who appreciate my rhyme.
I pour a flow of my verses like a draft
For transient, but forever thirsty time.

The ardent drummer-rain
Is knocking tango on my window.
It sounds like a long-distance train
That leaves behind a hint of innuendo.

Fiction

I am a child of doubts
And a protagonist of fiction
Confronted by the miracles of faith.

I am the one who went to see St. Paul
I am still alive; the angels missed my soul.

The rhythmic knocking of the wheels
And rather gentle rolling of the train,
Let go the annoying tasteless meals.
I hope the lasting trip is not in vain…

When I arrived, Paul was on vacation,
I overlooked his train, it left the station.

My future is unknown and unexplained,
It's like a tenebrous masterpiece,
Somewhat mysterious and luring…
My life is not a one-way street,
I am not a one trip pony,
I am not lost between he trees,
I am marching to my own beat,
As long as I remember, and even during
The heaven's unintended acrimony.

From Within

The fallen angel made a single ripple
In the small pool below my town digs,
I heard what said a passing stranger:
"The more I learn about people,
The more I like the pigs."

Nothing on Earth is free:
Sometimes, it's quid pro quo,
At times, it's the abyss or glee,
Now and then, it's ebb or flow…

The radiance of life
Comes from within;
It's not a quiet strife,
It's rather a break-in.

Enthusiastic Reader

Most books never escape their covers,
Only a few will reach our souls and brains.
Most books remind me of dog-tired lovers,
Or everlasting and pokerfaced, cold rains.

I am an enthusiastic reader
Of long obituaries in a local paper,
Just as a lack lustered undertaker,
Just as an ordinary bottom feeder.

I hold my own and sometimes thrive,
I outlived my doctors and most friends,
Only a few foes are still alive.
The means were justified by the ends.

It's not the time to kick the bucket,
It's not the time to buy the farm…
I found glee and safely lucked it,
Then threw away my radio alarm.

I hope to see another tender dawn,
The fear of a blue tomorrow is gone.

Gourmet Recipe

My wishes bounce
Off commonsense,
I am ready to denounce
My common self-defense.

I wasn't made from a tangible material,
I'm from the black-and-white cartoons,
I even failed to manage lowlife criteria;
Am I no better than the horrific goons
That suffer from verbal diarrhea,
And constipation of a good idea.

I see the answer looms:
There is a colossal gap
Between the poverty and money,
Between a diamond in the rough
And a drop of dirt in a sweet honey;
I wonder what's destined for my lap.

Only a conscious necessity
Becomes the ideal freedom,
It is a gourmet recipe
For choices if we ever need 'em.

Wicked Whiff

A prison of conformity
Makes an unending circle
Out of a nervous square …
Exactly like my wisdom,
Which is a pure deformity
Inherently feeble and infertile
Like a lackluster love affair.

Debates give birth to truth,
At large, the quarrels kill it.
I am fighting nail-and-tooth;
At times, I even use a skillet.

The moon rocks on the waves,
I walk toward the stony edge,
Toward the unforgiving cliff,
The tidy seagulls calmly sleep,
Their memory forever saves
All secrets of the enigmatic deep,
And only a short-lived wicked whiff
Friskily reminds me of my ripen age.

Stubbornly Unbowed

A typically raucous crowd
Was heading out of the traps;
Throwing at me their scraps,
But I was stubbornly unbowed
In route from peak-to-through
From a thickness to a thinness
Of my rundown bank account.
I'm a nerdish play-it-save man,
I coolly brush my problems off,
I have a different game plan,
I'm just sipping my Irish Guinness.

Some begged for help The Wailing Wall
Then flew away from our planet in despair,
Without an appointment to see St. Paul;
They thought that bliss is their pied a terre.

Nobody casually leaves to see St. Peter,
He rarely flies, but he isn't your babysitter.
Life over there isn't the daily quid-pro-quo,
Some carelessly reap what the others sow.

Fragile Kinshlp

I used to trust in harmony and friendship,
I used to trust in peace and coexistence.
But our inborn hostility's blind persistence
Aggressively destroys a fragile of kinship.

I live but have no other shoe to drop,
Reality is my nightmare,
Don't wake me up,
Don't let it stop.
I begged to pass by me that bitter cup,
There is no end to my despair,
Although, I still remember Mathew's verse,
I still enjoy the pulse of our wicked universe.

And yet, for trust,
I will be fooled,
For foolishness I will be gratefully trusted,
But only later understood and then disgusted.

Ultimate Inmate

I like myself, I left the gloom
Of convoluted circumstances.
I am a known-every-corner broom,
Nevertheless, I weigh his chances.

I am trying to untangle
Some of my interwoven strophes,
I veer and pivot, I twist and bend
My newest lyrics for Piazzolla' Libertango
With a farfetched hope for a few trophies.

I wish my pride and vanity will not prevail,
Eternal masquerade is over. I sold my vail.

I have a wicked sense of humor
Of a death row ultimate inmate,
I'm as funny as a deadly tumor
That entertaining my prostate…
My doctor pulled a rabbit from his hat:
You lived enough; this is your tit-for-tat.

Green

I never cared for money, fame and glory,
But after the popular ophthalmic surgery
That cured my dreadful sense of colors
And the others snags in my eye sockets,
I can no longer see our green dollars
In my beat-up wallet or tattered pockets.

Border Sheriff

I never drink alone,
I have to clink my glass
With someone else…
The name of a border sheriff
Inscribed on her tombstone…
Nobody gets arrested
For drinking or smoking grass.
We only heard the church's bells.

It was a cozy Spanish villa,
The game was worthy
Of contraband Tequila
On the gaming table…
I won enough
To tell the sheriff a cute fable
About her and my great love.

I didn't kill a drunken border sheriff,
She shot herself and didn't miss,
I only paid the highest tariff
For grass and that tequila,
She drank and smoked,
We couldn't even kiss,
She's dead. I walked.

Foggy Senses

As every poet, I wrote about red sunsets,
About cheerfully full of life sunrises,
Meanwhile, I place my mostly losing bets,
And toss the few coldblooded dices,
Despite my crumbling chanced
And rather foggy senses.

In modern life there is no common goal,
It's all about self-advancement,
It's all about aces in the hole,
It's all about drugs for self-enhancement.

When I will lose my final strife
And sorrowfully leave,
No one will cheer me at the gates of hell,
My bosom friends may even grieve.
Grief is a price for life,
And the unending memories to dwell.

No one can lift a fallen star,
It dies and leaves a ripple or a scar.

A Riddle

I bounce from each side
Of every talking mouth,
The truth stays in the middle,
I often fail to solve a riddle,
But try to be effective and dignified,
Exactly like the lucky second mouse.

My poetry is a nostalgic truth,
I'm trying to resurrect my past,
I'm dancing to the end of youth
With hope it will forever last.

Reasons

Our history is cruel and merciless
To our opinions and emotions;
It tromps through our commotions
And leaves them almost worthless.

Committing sins is our daily business,
At times, we even seek forgiveness
For a categorically clear reason:
We'll repeat the same another time;
Although, next time it may be prison
Which harshly turns us on a dime.

Hefty Drink

I wonder if it's a sparkling acting
Or I'm a smart and creative being,
Whether I'm fervent and attractive,
And comprehend what I'm seeing.

The pompous rhythms of marches
Don't lure my arthritic hips and legs
Into a sprightly daily walk.
I drag along the downtown arches
My worn-out trembling pegs
Into a happy hour at six o'clock.

I hate the scorching summers,
I like the breezy naughty morns
When the raindrops-drummers
March over the bending ferns
Poking a dew-sipping silence
With their infuriating thorns.

Time passes; the evening prowls,
The stars begin to blink,
The squirrels, bats, and owls
Hide in their cozy hollows…

I made for me a hefty drink.

Fig Leaf

My smile isn't a fig leaf
That covers my disillusions.
It hardly lulls my grief,
But multiplies confusions.

The key to being an adult
Is knowing what you like.
There is nobody to consult,
Just make a wish and strike.

Today, the Queen has died,
Long live the King!
The worthy next of kin.
I wish Charles a smooth ride
Across his troubled land
Of the eternal sin
Toward the happy end…

Morbid Wit

Most of the married men and women
Become noncompromising and cruel,
And like a stubborn rented mule:
Still argue what's first an egg or a hen.

There're too many busted marriages,
I wonder whether it is the Holy writ
Or Venus's winged Cupid's morbid wit;
I couldn't, at the moment, to say yes,
So, I finally gave up and hoofed it.

While I was in the hunt for answers,
I pivoted and veered like dancers,
And bumped into the weirdest faith:
I watched the souls of sinners bathe,
Not far away from where I live…

I gave you all my decency can give.

Lady Pig

I hoped this summer lasts forever,
But a cold autumn came and stayed
Without bad intentions whatsoever,
Granting, my fear of winters didn't fade.

It's not my winter yet,
I still have a few months to laugh,
I am not waiting for sunset;
The sun still hangs on my behalf.

To see the sun I cut some branches,
And even trimmed some leafy twigs…
Chess players wormed the benches
While I was dancing with a lady pig.

I end my life, and nothing is a secret,
Moreover, nothing is concealed;
I like this paradigm and try to keep it,
Although, my fated verdict isn't sealed.

Birthday

I am a hawk; I am not a raven,
I wouldn't seek a quiet haven,
I won't be destined for retreat,
Life is only a one-way street.

It is so strangely quiet,
No politics,
No scandals.
Today, I am eighty-six,
It's the first time I try it…
Two burning candles
Dripping on the table,
Is this a parting evening?
Is this a new beginning?
Is this a reality or just a fable?

Nightly Breeze

The first who pulls the gun
Is not the best or bravest,
He is the only one
Wearing a bulletproof vest.

He probably will see tomorrows
And he will get the key
From the evasive gates of glee
That may obliterate his sorrows.

He didn't lose a war
Before it started;
He locked the door
Reality departed.

The mine canary didn't sing,
He heard the siren's sound
And threw a towel in the ring;
He lost his first but final round.

The moon as a gigantic lantern
Pours light between the trees;
The shadows cast a lacy pattern
Caressed by the nightly breeze.

Great Sapphire

A real life delayed,
Just means a life denied.
That was a role I played
And left no trace behind.

Just mark my word,
I gather ashes of the new
That passed this world,
The heavens are still blue.

Our blue moon and stars
Look like a great sapphire
Surrounded with diamonds,
Wakes up my childhood desire
To fly as Icarus above the islands
Upwards the scorching sunny sky…

Today, nobody faces death alone:
We are accompanied by sultry fears,
By cheeses and a Pinot of Bourgogne,
And probably a keg of Belgian beers.

Too Often

At times, my poetry connects the dots,
I try to change this world,
I write, I chase a better word,
As if I pump the quarters in the slots.

Our desires rather untamed
And at no time domesticated;
A real love remains unnamed,
And our lives remain belated.

The words of love remain a lie,
Even the sweetest lie is deadly,
We know when to say goodbye
To those who treat us badly…
They likely wish you well,
They simply live in hell.

I'll die and will be burned,
My ashes will be "urned".
I don't deserve a pine top coffin,
I went to the abyss too often.

Canaries

I torture pages
Of my unfinished book
Seems through the ages;
They don't complain,
I let them go off the hook
Without "ball-and-chain".

We net our freethinkers like the fish,
They lose their dignity and health,
Some even do their time in prisons;
Canaries warned us in the mines
About these four major reasons:
The intellectuals just hope and wish,
The rich are fearful of losing wealth,
The middle classes have no spines,
The poor don't see the changes.

I am quite pessimistic for a while:
I see the future's cunning smile,
I watch the future's shifting eyes.

Our future is the devil in disguise.

Somber Night

Another night floats in a quiet river,
The stars dance with the fallen leaves,
The lonely crescent's feisty cleaver
Reminds me of my lifelong griefs,
And boldly flaunts its useless might.
I want to end this somber night.

The same night quietly descended
Upon the nameless graves
Of my comrades so cruelly handled:
The first, the young, the braves.

Children believe that lives don't end,
We know that our earthly lives finite,
For babies each of us is just a friend,
For us a sunny day becomes a night.

The moon treads water with its feet,
The darkest shadows split my street.

I Slept

I slept,
And asked the Lord
For a long easy life,
I should have asked
For a short easy death:
With purity of baby's breath
I craved to join him in my afterlife.

I slept,
The Devil stood at my bedside:
After a lengthily accusation,
The judge read ruling as a guide:
I had to choose between a suicide
And a cruel ritual immolation.
I could be burned at stake
Or could have a bullet in my heart;
Here comes the magic art,
I'll be forgiven in the wake.

I slept,
Drunk, naked and barefoot
Life wasn't lavish loot,
Life was a book,
Life was a stage,
I took a better look
And saw a written final page.

Literary Damper

My creativity in peril,
It is so hard to carve a line,
I write as if I am a barrel
Without a fermented wine.

The saints don't bother me,
God sent me to a sanctum;
I am safe and definitely free,
Today, I gratefully thanked him.

I write my lines in black-and-white,
Then digitally inject some colors
To sway the readers with the light
And see the portraits on the dollars.

I read my genuine four liners
To my deaf eared friends-diners,
And being a happy camper
I quickly lift their literary damper.

The show-life must go on,
The actors act and don't complain,
Long live the lifelong marathon!
Let's pop the bottle of champagne!

Tunnel Ended

I used to write about love forever,
About a shiny pair of golden rings,
About for the better and the worse,
But saw the angels with no wings,
The fools pretending to be clever,
And life that didn't echo any verse.

My mind too busy sharing trivialities,
My soul too busy handling banalities,
Rejected the comforts of suburban life;
My body totally and firmly disagreed:
Even in years gone by,
They saw nothing eye to eye,
They simply tore apart. Goodbye…

Back in the day,
I wore two velvet gloves,
Misled by the stars and loves;
I didn't fight,
I tried to sway,
I hoped to see the light…
The lifelong tunnel ended
And the darkness landed.

I wish I'd hold a pistol in my hand;
Then I could see the happy end.

Happy Eighth

I was susceptible to being paid,
Though, being player by my fate only,
And when I loved and wasn't lonely,
I still couldn't resist that poisoned bait.

Today, I am free,
I am not a hostage
Of my floating rhymes;
Today, I know glee,
I wouldn't hide my head
I am not an ostrich,
I am an eagle oftentimes.

I left the world of sunless days,
The world of endless competitions,
The world of constant chase,
The world of a naked greed
Reigned by the pitiless morticians.

A paradise is not a kingdom
Of the dead,
It is a known syndrome
Of ignoring our daily bread;
It is an insufficiency of faith,
It is not a deadly seventh sin,
It is a happy eighth,
Just next to kin.

Fishless Nets

The angels lead the brushes
Across my painting…
They stop when sunset blushes
And the sunbeams fainting.

I love the gloomy red sunsets,
Reflected in the ancient marbles,
Even the ashes, old and sparkles
Remind me of the fishless nets…

I scream about things
Some others only mumble,
I scream, but our future brings
The endless rough-and-tumble.

Homesick Traveler

I am a homesick traveler
Between the mysteries and dreams,
Between what's fair and what's unfair,
Across reality that's better than it seems

I walk the troughs and ridges
Under the seven colored bridges,
Of the sky-high wonder of a rainbow,
Along the Mississippi's pompous flow.

I bid farewell to Nashville, Tennessee
And moved to Arles, South of France.
As far as I could see
Life there is an ultimate romance,
At least, a paradise seems closer,
Than a busy traveler would think,
A barman like a shrewd composer,
Under the slowly passing moons
Pours a few just now written tunes
Into my skillfully shaken drinks.

Crying Candles

A nervous evening,
Two crying candles
On the dining table;
My friend is leaving:
I'm tired of her fable,
I cannot trust a word she says,
I hope to see much better days.

A watched pot never boils,
A good time for my doubts;
Only my body heartily toils,
Only my soul loudly shouts.

I'm given to understand:
That one can't enter
The same river twice,
But one can leave at once,
Just like a delinquent renter.
I wonder where I stand…

I can no longer trust
My daily pleasant dreams,
I trust only my dire nightmares;
They try to stop my love affairs,
And I will cease them if I must.

Nobody Follows

The stars hide in the hollows
Of our daytime flawless skies.
It's all in vain, nobody follows
My admonitions and my cries.

My peers' aristocratic wreckage
Was hailed by the nouveau riche,
They gleamed in a reflected light
From the olden myths and fables;
They lived in a cocoon of greed
Until they got a caution message
That they will see the empty dish,
That they will lose their final fight
Far in the sky, above the gables,
After the godsent truth succeeds.

Don't ever look for me
Between the ancient graves,
I am still alive above the ground,
I try to square my worldly round,
Meanwhile, I still enjoy my glee.

When someone dies, God saves.

Crystal Ball

A crystal ball foretelling life,
Foreseeing our days ahead,
Lies shattered on the floor,
Still pure as Caesar's wife,
Still flawlessly keeps score,
But has been left for dead.

The ball revealed its secrets,
Predicted gains and losses,
Saw a hysteria or sequence
In our managers and bosses.

I see a silent ball, no paradigm:
Ten pennies don't make a dime,
And only the ear bursting silence
Enjoys finances' pseudoscience.

Too Far

A man who can't admit his guilt
Reminds me of a bridge
That was completely burned
But then rebuilt.
Reminds me of the sun
That rolled beyond the ridge,
Reminds me of a life
That was at the time adjourned.

I spent three days
Away from home, in the abyss;
No one can trace
My trip away from a daily bliss;
It was a total lack of good,
It was a total dominance of evil,
I didn't have to knock on wood.
I lived in time of great upheaval.

The stars danced tango in the skies,
And didn't pay attention to our fray
For glory of the stars-and-bars;
I healed my wounds and scars…
Today, I walk in spite of feet of clay
Toward my own deliberate demise.

I may become a star
After my timely death;
The fallen angel is too far
Away and under my final breath.

Quiet Dove

A friendship can be earned,
But love is a lesson learned.
The youngsters sleep
With whom they love,
We sowed what they reap.
The gray-haired love
With whom they sleep.
A gutsy but worn-out hawk
Becomes a quiet dove.

My wisdom studies from the past,
And scratches its attractive layer…
Maybe it's all useless and in vain,
Maybe the memories won't last,
Like tunes on a worn-out player
That lingered like a chronic pain.

The hostile youth is booming,
My dire frustrations looming;
I'd rather die and rest in peace
Than live forever on my knees.

Eerie Smokes

I write with broad brushstrokes,
Impulsively avoiding thin nuances,
I see my life through eerie smokes,
And shots of tequila's lovely ounces.

My life is a constant "happy hour"
Or just a whisker off that bliss;
I am obliged to live life to the fullest
And hardly guzzle my brainpower
To dodge the whistling bullets…
My critics fortunately often miss.

I don't expect pennies from heaven,
And I don't get the shiny quarters,
I have no time to tread the waters.
I happily commit the mortal seven.

Experience is a bloodsucking leech,
The ages gone don't ever teach,
They only comfort our idle brains,
They justify our fiascos and mistakes,
They bounce all the modern gains,
They try to eat and have their stakes.

The Bucket

Perhaps, there was a god,
Who knew the primal word.
But I sincerely doubt
That we'll ever find out
Where he may tuck it.

We shun the lightning rod,
Or we may kick the bucket.

Unique Concern

I don't deserve forgiveness,
I am not familiar with remorse,
Confession is a chronic illness
As wearing as a bad divorce...

I give advice to gullible bystanders
About virtues and their upper prices,
I tout them what met my standards,
I am distressed by fruitless sacrifices.

I am not afraid
To keep on living,
Still loving and still giving
I throw a Frisbee to my dog,
He runs like a teenager to a date,
He jumps just like a springtime frog,
And crows like a minor who's got laid.

My life is quite a journey far from over,
I drink a lot but if I am more-less sober
I face a nagging and a unique concern:
To borrow or to earn,
To cross the bridge
Or let it burn?

Great Divides

The nightly skies look hollow
When demons hide the stars,
Meanwhile, the barflies follow
My journeys through the bars.

I am a friend of angels,
I am a friend of demons;
Sometimes I let them fight
Between the happy hours;
No one is ever wrong or right,
They both are falling powers.

They are two equal sides
Of the same ancient coin,
They are two great divides,
But each is trying to purloin
Our treasure known as a life,
Our never netted falling knife.

Awfully Brittle

What doesn't kill,
Will make you stronger...
The engineers of our lives,
The pedagogical contractors,
The pitiless redactors,
The literary housewives,
Our censors are still wrong
And try to get much wronger.

My thin-skinned critic
Old, bitter, and arthritic,
Replaced his rusty guns
With hatred, ink, and spittle.
I firmly stated: kiss my buns;
His ego was awfully brittle
And he committed suicide.
I didn't kill him, thou I tried.

Near Me

There's a cinema near me;
I went to see the show
Named "The Wisdom Tree",
It taught me all I know.

The crying masks of tragedy,
The laughing masks of comedy
Remind me of a vanity parade,
Recaps a Venetian masquerade.

Who are beyond the masks?
Nobody guesses this charade,
We are all equal in the casks,
Nobody gets a higher grade.

The Letter

I wrote an honest poem of despair,
I sealed and stamped the envelope,
But didn't send to editors the letter,
I think I still caressed my hope
Io see my days as fair-and-square,
To see this world a little better...

At last, I am carried
Into the middleclass fragility
By my good fortune or by ability,
I'll take both; I'm not yet married.

Most of the times,
The poems I amassed
Send streams of dissent rhymes
Into the future from my sunny past.

The night and day collide,
The stars abruptly hide
In the alluring hollows
Of the morning skies,
But no one follows;

They will routinely rise
Before the next sunrise.

My Existence

I am a student of masterpieces
Of the olden Greco-Roman art,
It is the brick-and-mortar
Of my existence;
I make this easy for my heart
To tap along a lifetime distance.

I learn the walk of our world
From the first row,
Not from the dusty books,
I owe that seat a major part
Of what I ever knew or know,
It is much better than it looks.

It moves so fast,
I miss it when I blink;
In spite of a gloomy overcast,
I wouldn't miss it when I think.

Life

My life is fairly squared,
It lulls before the storm;
I am quite well prepared,
I wear my navy uniform.

Life sees my future
In the rearview mirror,
At dawn,
She is a merciless butcher,
At night,
She is a converted cheerer.
At noon,
Like every public pleaser
Life is a bird of paradise,
At dusk,
She is a flightless teaser
For our sleepy, idle eyes.

I know life enough
To see what's right,
But not enough
To see what's wrong.
At times,
Life leads you to the light,
But takes you for a song.

Daily Yarn

I saw a dawn in mourning,
She said, the last sunset
Was a friendly warning
That hopes are gone…

Hopes soar,
Hopes plunge;
I write my verses,
Meanwhile, those horses,
The dire apocalyptic four
Enjoy our no-way-out grunge.

Our horses left the stable,
Our own cows left the barn;
I sipped my brandy at the table,
My girlfriend gave a daily yarn.

I locked the squeaky door
Into my want-to-see you past,
Then called my bosom friend
And yelped, come over fast.
He came and I began to pour
The rarest most expensive wine;
We live, no matter rain-or-shine.
It's not the end…

Augean Stables

They say a beggar
Can't be a chooser;
I chose to live as a bootlegger,
I generally hate to be a loser…

Nevertheless, quite often,
I clean somebody's stables,
I wipe away somebody's sins
Until they dive into a coffin…
My fortune constantly enables
Me to see where it all begins;
The enemy is us:
By our luck or by God's inability
We weren't pushed under the bus.

Long live our over-all natural futility!

Espresso

I drink a lot
As if I am a thirsty fish.
I have a sacred wish
To tear the Gordian knot
Of our medical wellbeing.

I trust in a heavy drinking
And an excessive peeing.

For a good digestion
I drink a darker beer,
For a good appetite
I drink white wine,
To raise blood pressure
I drink cognac or espresso,
To lower a blood pressure
I gobble down my red wine,
I sip chilled vodka or tequila
Against a bad cold or covid.

You asked do I drink water.
I have no illness for it.

Brown Eyes

Life is a living holiday
That follows me,
Life is a drunken glee;
I'd hate to pass away…

I drown in the sea of love,
I drown in your brown eyes,
My heart is set on fire
In the sea above,
Am I in paradise
Where is all the angel's art?
Not yet,
I'm falling from the skies.

Parisian Smells

I veer through a red river
Of the cars ahead of me.
I have an awesome fever
I am in Paris; I am in glee.

I love the smells of Paris-town,
Each smell is a precious souvenir,
It's like the odor of my mother's gown,
So unforgettable, so cordially dear.

The smell of a cigarette
And a spit-out butt,
The smell of a genuine omelet,
The smell of a sautéed chestnut,
The smell of a French perfume
The smell of a tourist bus's fume,
The smell of the springtime roses,
The naked gods provoking poses,
The tempting smell of making love…

It is the end, I wrote enough.

Spooked

I ate my turf-and-surf
And hoped to be in heaven;
The steak was overcooked,
The lobster was alive,
Didn't commit those seven,
But felt entirely spooked;
I need a really cooking wife.

My dog-days didn't pour,
They only rained…
I made half-baked decisions,
No principals, no visions,
And quickly lost
What I so laboriously gained.

I lost my trust in friends,
I lost my rainbow-hued illusions,
I lost my doubts and confusions,
I lost my hope for happy ends.

Ripened Figs

Unlike a naughty loud science
Of a chaotic students' dorm,
I lived in a ghostly total silence
In the eye of a springtime storm.

Surrounded with a constant danger
Of brutal competitions and intrigues,
I learned to live like a fallen angel,
I learned to be somewhat malicious;
I picked a low hanging fruit.
She was one of the juicy, ripened figs,
She was extremely cute,
She was incredibly delicious.

We usually take the best life offers,
Some get the casks,
The others get the coffins;
Some joyfully wear the masks
For the Venetian masquerades,
The others die from HIV and AIDS,
Some find the early treasure troves,
The others put their heads in stoves.

Forgot

My mind's unwavering desire
To comb through the unknown,
Reminds me of a fading fire
After a candle wick was blown.

From time to time I miss,
I can't imagine or recall a lot:
I accurately crossed the t's,
I didn't dot the i's; I just forgot.

I was a needle in a haystack,
I didn't think of a brass plaque
On my run-down house's wall,
With a few golden letters:
Here lived a great poet Paul.

Perhaps these days it matters.

Wish

My baldheaded selfish youth
Morphed into a bearded aging,
And in the pursuit of a naked truth,
I didn't escape a pompous staging,
And reaped a plentiful applause...
I have arrived,
My deed usurped me in its claws.
Reality contrived
I never met a single class of people
That's greedier than nouveau riche,
The so-called former stone-broke...
Although, it's wrapped in spittle,
I have a modest wish:
"Leave me alone, go up in smoke".

So Long

There is no truth without a debate,
Thus if and when you disagree,
Convincingly present your view,
Whether it is provocative and new,
Just pull your horns and wait,
Truth is a jewel, nobody gets it free.

Perhaps, it doesn't matter in a way,
But every night all cats look gray;
The silhouettes of hawks or doves
Against a dark sky, look the same;
In time, even our everlasting loves
Become completely lame…

The sun will always rise,
I wonder, when the sunny ray
May close its eyes and sleep,
Or close its eyes and pray,
Or throw its never lucky dice
And weep.

Meanwhile, I tortured my guitar,
Nobody liked my poetry and song;
I felt just like a hopeless falling star,
But made a heartfelt wish:" So long".

Human Lives

I study human lives,
I have no other aim or thought,
Nor take up any other thing to study,
But our world and its godsent paradigm:
I visit beers-and-billiard dives,
I write about drunkards and barflies;
I never bought or fought
Any idea that looked unclear or muddy,
I knew a better way to waste my time.

I study human lives:
Some suffered and then died,
The others thrived
And lived in their golden digs;
Nothing will ever change,
Life was and is a shooting range.
The more I learn about human lives,
The more I love the snakes and pigs.

Innuendo

My critics gather at my window,
Then fade somewhere at night,
But leave a poisoned innuendo
About everything I say or write.

I am a birthright inevitable poet
Encircled by these acidic critics,
And tailed by many runners-up;
They are like those mushrooms
That pop after each rainy morning
Around ugly piles of bosh and mud,
But loved by the so-called analytics.
Besides, our theatre-life must go on
They play the only given to them role,
They bore to death my mind and blood.

Another Epigram

We eagerly correct the errors of the others,
But hardly know how not to err;
Nobody tries, nobody bothers
To recognize their faces in the mirrors,
To see what's fair and what's unfair,
To separate the villains from the heroes.

Old Epigram

The darkest caves
Of our souls,
The narrow roads
Of our minds,
Rest in the quiet graves
With drawn down blinds,
Behind the secret codes.

Dead actors have no roles.

Epigram

I calmly woke this morning
Alone, without anybody near,
I knew, it was a timely warning,
It was up-to-date Paul Revere:
"Your loneliness is coming,
Your loneliness is coming,
Don't wait, keep running!!!"

Lifer

Life mentioned all my rights,
But didn't ask a single question;
She knew that I will take the fifth
To stay away from traps and fights;
My hopes had just that final bastion
As isle in the quagmire of daily filth.

A New Year even in jail
Supposed to be a Happy Year;
Although, life is a cruel prison
In which I am a lifer locked forever;
A brutal frost as our Lord arisen
Draws my future on a window,
A cunning picture, a lacy innuendo,
A never-ending convoluted fear
Of my ill-timed demise without bail,
Without any mercy, whatsoever.

Today, life dipped her toes
In my often unworthy thoughts
About aloof friends and bosom foes,
Who fight like Jason's Argonauts,
Committing cruelty in self-defense,
All in the myths of Zeus' created past.

For me life's waffle has no future tense,
No sun, but only a melancholy overcast.

Cherries

Two full of tourists riverbanks,
Two friendly marble parallels,
One swirling muddy Arno River,
One Ponte Vecchio's gold fever
Fanned by the greed driven caravels;
I like the fated Florence' Midas touch,
Forever fast or loud, never too much.

Duomo, David, and Uffizi are three cherries,
Or rather an overwhelming icing on the cake,
The crown of the grandeur Florence carries,
That keeps me mystified and wide-awake.

I wasn't taught by the ancient writers,
I write my folksy red-blooded limericks,
I often echo the coarse streetfighters
I am a basic mortar between the bricks.
I carve my rather good-natured strophes,
But never get to own the polished trophies.

Some say, our fame is similar to death,
It borrows us from relatives and friends,
It loans us arrogance and a heavy breath,
And leaves us with the futile odds and ends.

Broken Mast

A friendship gained
Not through grandeur
And nobility of spirit
Is earned but cannot last;
It's like a sailboat
With a broken mast:
We can't navigate,
But only rock and veer it,
Just as the stubborn mules.

Welcome to a ship of fools.

Santa

This is what my life is all about:
I try to keep my eyes wide open,
I desperately need to figure out
Where rubber meets the road,
I want to learn the secret sauce;
Maybe, in vain, I am still hoping
To click a photo and download
The one, the real Santa Clause.

Thorns

Under the most legendary star
Melchior, Gaspar and Balthazar
Found a little town Bethlehem,
And launched our eternal mayhem.

Undying quarrels killed the dragons,
The circling of the wagons
Won't help in modern times;
Life is a crown of the sharpest thorns,
These days, we simply pull our horns
And penetrate the innocence of crimes.

Abandoned Craters

Receding rows of skyscrapers
Have risen from the dreams
Of those who later landed
On our moon's abandoned craters;
And thoughts have been expended,
Enlightened by the sunny beams.

I walk in my buttoned-down coat
Across the New-York Central park,
The birds stopped singing every note
Written by glowing radiance of light;
They saw the terrifying depths of dark
And jumped into the looming night.

My curiosity doesn't allow me to croak,
I gained insights from silliness of others,
I tried to morph each trouble into a joke
And hedged myself from all that bothers.

My life's experience is a chronic illness
Without any pills or cures on the horizon,
It is my intellectual unending stillness
Without any possibility to wisen.

The history can only see the past,
I hope, God's angels can forecast.

A Gap

I will keep dancing,
The melody is on,
I am already facing
My farewell dawn.

I wish I had a father
Who didn't drink so much,
I had a perfect mother,
She was a real saint,
If they exist as such,

What's good for the geese
Is good for a gander,
I'll enjoy my life, I won't surrender;
The second mouse gets the cheese.

No one can jump across a gap
In two half-jumps.
What is a price of victory and fame?
We jump over the tongues of flame,
And reach the edge of glory.
The end of race. The end of story.

Ailment

I trawl my happy days in muddy waters,
I raised some pennies, but no quarters.

I witnessed bloody fights
Between my thoughts
Entirely opposite at times,
I saw the darkness killed the lights,
I saw the never-ending crimes
Under the handmade quilts of nights.

Take off your mask,
And you will face the truth;
It's different for everyone
But what's beyond?
A chaos, a nightmare, a void?
Take my advice:
The truth in only known to the Lord,
I plow my mind,
I search for a new idea,
I still am empty-handed,
There is no cure, no panacea
For ailment, that is unbranded.

Bagels

My healthy senses of right and wrong,
So far, refuse to sing the parting song,
I realize, some get delicious bagels,
The others only get the holes,
Some wear huge diamonds and sables,
The others fight and die in their foxholes.

The wheel of time
Rolls slowly through the Milky Way
From a shiny dollar to a soiled dime,
Meanwhile, my agonizing conscience
Would never hesitate to say:
"One can't eat principles for dinner
In our enamored life,
Be dignified, you'll become a winner,
And never lose your lifelong strife."

Beer Truck

I used to be a seaman,
I used to sail too long;
My wife arranged to see a man,
And learned to sing that oldest song.

Another careless night
Turned off the blinking stars,
Life sunk into a hazy sadness;
I had to drug my yoke of badness,
I had to lull my life. I went to fight
My barflies-buddies in the local bars.

I live in a shambolic world
As every Brit would say:
When justice is derailed
My sweet delusions fade
Unless I am above the fray;
When justice is denied
Reality is pushed aside,
I sell my soul and body for a buck
And veer like a runaway beer truck.

I've been worn down by my past,
By marriages that didn't last,
By inability to live a proper life…
Instead of peace I'd choose a strife.

Bottom Line

The quirky flashbacks revive my strife,
I used to be a brainless cannon fodder,
A total imbecile, a gullible applauder;
The leaders pledged a cloudless life.

We all were victims of a sneaky plot
And failed to slash the Gordian knot.

Why am I descending on an elevator?
Why am I ascending from a quarry?
Why am I climbing from a crater?
None of the above makes any sense,
Perhaps, it's just a poetic allegory…
That states I march beyond the fence.

I'd rather grade my earnest efforts,
The others grade only the bottom line.
What will be graded by the final court?

I won't see heaven after a lifelong race.
But …just in case.

Ceaseless Marathon

The gifts our Almighty sends
Look like the bloody slaughters.
No one is hiding in the corners
I went to war with friends,
We heard and calmed the mourners,
But knew wars umpired by the ends.

The door into my life is bolted,
No one gets over there;
My heartbeat is for a moment halted,
Because I can no longer bear
Even a slim necessity to coexist
With kids who never heard
Of Chubby Checker!
They never danced his famous twist,
And every living nerd
Believes it was a digital spell-checker.

My poetry is just a map
Of never-ending ends,
It looks like a quilt of puzzles.
I comb through them alone
Without relatives or friends;
Only my dream still dazzles.

I run my ceaseless marathon.

The tide of grief
Lifts every boat…
I simply wonder if
Our deeds still float.

Compared

A poet wannabe,
A movie star who didn't make it,
A girl who whispers yes,
But never no or maybe,
The worshipers who don't believe
But learned to fake it…
I say hello and shake their hands,
Are they acquaintances or friends?

My poetry is duly noted
By many of my friends
Who bought my books.
I never wanted them
To be the mindless fish
Hung on my hooks.

I'm fighting-writing tooth-and-nail,
I keep the winds in my poetic sail.

I didn't bubble in hilarity
Like some excited fish,
But I admit with all sincerity,
I've been a little bit standoffish.
I have received a great response
For my most recent book:
I was big-heartedly compared
With masters of the Renaissance.

I hope, I didn't bite the luring hook.

Daily Yarn

I saw a dawn in mourning,
She said, the last sunset
Was a friendly warning
That hopes are gone…

Hopes soar,
Hopes plunge;
I write my verses,
Meanwhile, those horses,
The dire apocalyptic four
Enjoy our no-way-out grunge.

Our horses left the stable,
Our own cows left the barn;
I sipped my brandy at the table,
My girlfriend gave a daily yarn.

I locked the squeaky door
Into my want-to-see you past,
Then called my bosom friend
And yelped, come over fast.
He came and I began to pour
The rarest most expensive wine;
We live, no matter rain-or-shine.
It's not the end…

Eighty-Six

I am eighty-six,
I am spoiled by my luscious wines,
I see, I hear, I walk, I run, I even drive,
But hardly pay attention to the signs.
I have some other wholesome tricks
To keep my energies alive…
I write my verse and play some chess.

I am not familiar with remorse,
I am not familiar with confessions,
I'd rather write another moody verse,
I'd rather satisfy my weird obsessions.

I like to march against the streams,
I often argue with the powerholders,
I try to push uphill my better dreams,
In vain, just like Sisyphean boulders.

Erratic Sky

Pass by, don't envy, and forgive my glee,
I know wounds and pain; I know anguish,
I have a troubled life, but never languish,
I am still fighting; I never planned to flee.

I live under the blue, but an erratic sky,
Without any gods,
Without any angels,
Without any saints,
But stabbed by the bright lightning rods;
They loudly enlighten me and strangers
By bending the rainbows' seven paints.

Right out of the gate,
I am veering on feet of clay,
I am a head and shoulders
Above the unrelenting fray.

I see the Sisyphean huge boulders,
Somebody placed them in my fate…
Dusk morphed into the night,
No colors; all is black and white.
I am betrayed; I can no longer write.

Exhausted Soul

Under the long bent necks
Of chandeliers and torchers,
The slyly stacked new decks,
Dealt by another heartless night;
Between depression and delight,
In search of our ambiguous goals
We lose our pride and fortunes,
We tarnish our exhausted souls.

One day, in vain, late in my life,
I questioned, I tried to understand,
Why do I walk as a one-man-band?
Why do I march from strife to strife?
Why can't I live a day of peace?
Why can't I see the forest for the trees?

I am tirelessly winding on my wheels
The endless tape of highways' miles,
I wolf the low-cost meat-and-two meals,
I like to see the truck stop hookers' smiles.

I reenact the same worn-out roles,
I sense a void between two poles.

Fallen Heroes

A moderator introduced the speakers
And briefly outlined their views;
A bunch doubtful truth-seekers
Caressed their knowledge of the news
Injected into their ethereal religions
And sounded like emptyheaded pigeons,
Who knew the answers for the questions
And dared to mumble some suggestions.

The speakers sited the abyss and paradise,
But truth instantly drowned in the sea of lies.

Futility of that debate
Was greatly elevated
I easily rebuffed the bait
And I was also overrated.

It was quite obvious to me,
I knew a faster path to glee.

We cannot see our past in dusty mirrors,
Only the shiny ones reflect the real truth,
And show us the fallen heroes
Of our childhoods and youths.

Fermented

I am belonging to a threatened era,
I am as rare as rains in the Sahara.

Only my critics noisily lamented
That I am a juicy grape that is fermented
Into the mystery of life and love,
Demanding but extremely gentle,
Forever passionate and sentimental
Just like an iron fist in a velvet glove.

It was a bumpy journey, not a destination,
Like ancient Abraham and Sarah,
I reached the pinnacle of glee
After the empty trains have left the station.

It's written in the wind,
I lived and often sinned,
I saw tomorrows taking shape…
Today, I am asking Thee:
Will I be forgiven or cruelly pinned?

Flying Kites

I liked to watch the flying kites,
The painted long-tailed dragons,
My tender childhood dreams
That veered lit by the sunny beams.

They used to disappear at nights,
Into our parents' station wagons.

Tonight, my loneliness and I,
Both sit at the front row table,
And want a stripper to drop her dress,
Just like a tree that sheds its leaves;
The drunken moon hangs on a gable,
And I am too, a little high,
A little bit unstable,
But I remember my address,
Unless my trusted memory deceives.

Forgotten Art

Even the most flattering self-portraits
Will not let go premonition of the end,
Even a critic-genius will not interpret
The meaning of a red line in the sand.

I saw ascending waterfalls of lights,
I saw descending sparking fireworks,
I lived through the horrific wartime nights
When rockets pop like Champagne corks.

The nights of jarring color combinations,
The nights of black-and-white collisions
Entirely disregarded limits of my visions
And overstepped my damaged patience.

Long shadows whispered gentle lullabies,
I tried to sleep and closed my weary eyes,
Then soared into the castle in the skies
And let the future cast the dice
Into a young and trembling dawn;
Life will not fail to go on
And cupids will not miss my heart.

In war love was a well forgotten art.

Genetics

We are genetically inclined
To disregard the boundaries,
And to overshoot the fences.
We trail whims of our mind
Over the foreign countries,
Above the common senses.

.

But then life pulls the reins
And our genetics disappear:
We're meant to sip champagne,
But guzzle the most ordinary beer.

Good living is a complicated art,
It's a whole tour, not just a start.

Just send a warm goodbye
To insecure genetics and DNA;
They offered us our initial "A",
We have to make it to the "Y".

Golden Dime

My flesh had pompous burial today,
My soul is not expecting to survive;
I used to write about those who sinned,
Confessed and then forgave themselves,
About those who have no time to pray,
About those who work from eight to five;
Their sails already grabbed the wind
And they are judging someone else.

My style has undergone
My critics' literary slaughters,
My style has undergone the test of time;
Don't throw your poet out with the water,
Among the wimpy silver quarters
I am the only hearty golden dime.

He Winked

My life has been a thousand missteps,
I crossed too many lines,
I didn't pay attention to the hedges,
I've seen forgiven and forgotten debts,
Meanwhile I carved my humble lines,
And didn't waste my empty pledges.

It wasn't just a pocket change,
It was my all-hands-on-deck life,
It was a brutal, noisy shooting range
From eight to five
Before the sleepless nights,
And then, again the futile fights.

I was the devil's advocate,
As long as he is free,
I'd get my cut
And hid his shady pedigree
Of a noncompliant Lucifer,
Who used to be the brightest angel,
But fell and missed the sweet affair,
The star of Bethlehem and Jesus' manger.

Imaginary Wins

"Demands of our thankfulness
Are worse than thanklessness."

This great idea caught me by surprise
Then vanished on a never dusted page
As if the sun on a whim refused to rise
And a gentle dawn won't leave its cage.

In spite of our wealth or fame,
We always need some quarters
To enter our life's slot machines
And get our frequent losses
After our imaginary wins.

I am devoured by the gambling flame
That even burns God-given daily bread;
I am the needle, greed is the thread,
I move ahead and take the blame.

Infinity

I hear: "infinity will end quite soon…
Don't miss another passing moon."
That song was hanging in the air
Like an annoying hair
Of my morning biscuit,
But I am in a wicked mood
And hate to risk it.

It is a dreamy blast
Into my naughty past;
The music numbs my sighs,
I close my dreamy eyes
To see my footprints
On the scene of many crimes.
I'm a frog but used to be a prince;
So many moons passed by,
I waved my infinite goodbye
And haven't been there since.

Fortunately, today I know:
"Infinity will end quite soon…
Even the memories may kill…
Sandbags won't stop its flow."
It's all I learned,
I think it is a time to write my will,
The bridge into my past is burned.

Kitchen Sink

I am a kitchen sink
For my good friends,
They dump in me their sorrows,
Even their souls and minds;
I calculate the odds and link
Their past and their tomorrows;
I selflessly cheer up their moods,
I walk them through the woods,
I rinse delusions, help the blinds.

The more I knew about human beings,
The more I disapproved their dealings.

The wick was burning on my candle,
I've been forever a straight shooter,
I craved the truth, a few could handle.
I tried to clip their pride just as a looter.
With what I didn't like, I meddled,
To no avail, I brazenly back-pedaled.

Like a chameleon, I changed my hues,
But kept alive my genuine, clear views.

Linguistic Pulp

My verse is a silent mime,
Or just a linguistic pulp
And rubbish on a silver tray;
It's rather a bad time
To sip my coffee cup
And start another day.

And yet, another day, another love affair,
We are entering my comfy pied-a-terre,
She is a gorgeous lady of old pedigree;
Despite the elevated risk of birth defects,
She desperately craves a child from me;
She drops her skirt and personal effects,
No whisper, no foreplay, just a naked lust;
Sex is forever a fervent out-and-out must.

Millennials

Millennials remind me of thirsty flowers,
I often fertilize their thirsty roots,
God sends them hefty showers,
And yet, I seldom see green shoots.

Life aims its vicious Tasers
Between their trembling shoulders,
And hits them as the sharpest razors
Before the eyes of totally inert beholders.

I like to orchestrate my views,
I listen to advices, take the cues,
I had postponed my inevitable death,
To halt millennials from taking a final breath.

Much Younger

A cloud of disappointment
Hangs just above my head,
I missed our Lord's appointment,
I wasn't ready for the final flight,
I write, I am not yet dead,
When life's worth living, I will fight.

My angel went to check the Hell,
Like our Jesus, only for a day,
Without him I am still living well,
I eat and drink-no time to pray.

Each year when springs arrive,
The world becomes much younger:
We dance and sing, we thrive,
We rarely twist our tongue in anger.

A circle doesn't start and doesn't end,
It's like a dart that cupid didn't send,
But we are waiting for a real love,
Often forever as for all of the above.
Untiringly as for the all from the above.

My Tale

My memory is not a rusty nail
On which I hang my written pages;
It is my uneasy, happy life, it is my tale,
It is my honest portrait painted for the ages.

.

Naughty Wink

Just a few minutes to lie down,
That's what a truly need.
I let my soul and body drown
Before I sowed my final seed.

My verses helped me to remember
That golden fish, I netted in the sea,
A god of water Neptune was a sender,
She offered me only a meat and three.

No luck; I needed to pull-in my horns,
I didn't want to wear a wreath of thorns.

A horrible flatfooted merciless day
Was quite impatient at my door,
I wrote a scenario for this vile play,
Correctly named "My Farewell War".

The judge decreed to take my life,
My birthright and my only treasure.
I gave him back my naughty wink,
My vanity's grace under pressure.
I lost my final strife.
The verdict didn't have to dry its ink.

Name Engraved

I am astounded by the view:
The autumn trees wear golden gown,
The raging sultry sun
Hangs in the blue-veiled endless sky.

I walk the lifelong avenue,
A road that sooner or later ends,
But I am already sliding down,
Passing my foes and friends.

My girlfriend whined
That I am incredibly annoying.
Oh, well; I lived and learned,
The bridge into the future
Is already burned.

There's nothing wrong
From where I sit,
She let me sing my song
And life got lit.
It was another love
That held us long enough.
She whispered lovingly to me:
"Enjoy the moment. It is glee:"

I flew over a marble stone
With a familiar name engraved,
And realized, I am not a clone,
I am forever saved…

Oops

It sounds like a broken record,
But I am that dog, who caught a bus,
And quickly learned that enemy is us:
There are no tickets to get in,
No one can climb aboard,
In our daily walk, the ice that's awfully thin.

The doors of our souls are open wide,
We stand against the sky-high walls,
The fallen angel is our thoughtful guide:
Act like the devils at the gate,
Just shoot, don't ever wait;
The smart and dedicated rarely win,
Victorious are not the brave or passionate
Victorious are those who blindly obstinate
Who easily can take it on the chin.

We listen to the fairytales about heroes,
We see their smiling faces in the mirrors,
We learn their sugarcoated deeds,
But they annoy us as the backyard weeds.

We are still jumping through the hoops,
Just like the circus' dogs;
We are the princesses and princes
Lovingly kissed and turned into the frogs.
Oops.

Pinnacle

I am from another era…
Just like a juicy grape,
I was fermented into the mystery of life.

It is a bumpy journey, not a destination,
Like ancient Abraham and Sarah,
I'll reach my pinnacle and glee
After the trains have left the station.

It's written in the wind,
I see tomorrows taking shape,
And I am asking Thee:
Will I be forgiven?
Will I be pinned?

Protracted Childhood

I am so happy with my choice,
Which is my other, naughty side:
I bought a fabulous Rolls-Royce,
The finest bad-ass ride.

I am faithfully remaining
On the cusp of young adulthood:
I wouldn't shoot, I am just aiming
At my reclining wisdom and maturity,
Away from a sweltering obscurity
Of my willfully protracted childhood.

I bet, it is a bourgeois mentality
That shares its fated boredom
Of a blasé, monotonous reality
With my new gold-plated home.

Remember This

I drink my whiskey from a firehose,
I balance a huge piano on my nose,
I even learned to square the circles.
In politics I shun the reds and blues,
I close my eyes and bear the purples.

We, who survived explosions
Of the folic-shaped ballistic rackets,
Often end up in the psychiatric clinics,
And suffer from the tight embraces
Of the irrational straightjackets.

In spite of the darkest skies,
Despite the upbeat future-telling stars,
Regardless of the doctors' lies…
War said: "You will remember this,
Nobody can erase your memories
Of bloody wounds and hide your scars."

Roman Holiday

Our gray-haired bus
Crept over the narrow streets
Of the eternal Rome;
There were about twelve of us,
Stuffed like sardines in our seats,
Yet, gawking at the Peter's dome.

We bought some costly tickets
To see the greatest show
Of our long-lasting holiday:
Although, through tiny wickets,
The clergy let us see the glow
Over the head of John the Baptist,
Quietly resting on the famous tray.

No infamy; we were the tourists,
We were the shameless beasts.

It is no brainer,
We put John's head over his skis;
Back home we'll need a strainer
To separate integrity from sleaze.

Steering Wheel

Poetic waters are quite choppy
But I have learned, in any rate:
Bad poets copy,
Good poets imitate,
Great poets steal.
I, so called, turn my steering wheel,
I write my humble poetry and wait,
I never knew my birthright fate;
But I'm driven by the work of others
Into the band of my poetic brothers.

My bubbly life of chances
Continuously misses
Good fortune's hugs and kisses
Improving my personal finances.

Even my kids and babysitters
Besides my cats and dogs
Loathed businessmen with jitters
And reps with bags and catalogues.

Today, the guardrails are in place,
I am in the pleasure seeking race,
I wander toward the horn of plenty
Across the Andrew Jackson twenty.

Ten Inches

I finally arrived to this cold truth:
We relish our happy childhoods,
At times, we have a pretty youth,
Then come the years of lies,
The years of our mothers' cries,
That stay in filthy neighborhoods.

Each one has bragging rights,
That we politely seldom use.
While young, we daily took
The carnal knowledge bites;
Even I was daily making love
To my never-say-no muse.

Each one who has the guts
Enjoys a life; alternative is dire.
We used to pull the chestnuts
From the razorblades of fire,
Just to undress the juicy girls,
Nobody used ten inches pearls.

Three Apples

It was a tailwind for all,
I dumped my disillusions
Into the kitchen sink,
And listened to a cuckoo bird
That counted the years
Remain with me to laugh and drink.

I wanted to discuss some issues
With our Lord who art in the sky.
I am overly emotional, I often cry,
So, I will bring with me soft tissues.

Three apples changed our world:
The most delicious was bit by Eve,
The other fell on Isaac Newton's head,
The third was invented by Steve Jobs.
Times squeezed us through a sieve
And our bodies disagree with gluten,
But we have learned to push the knobs.

The real truth seems credible,
If it is wrapped in a quilt of lies,
Both colorful and spreadable
Like the abundant fields of paradise.

Tomorrows

Tomorrows of my past
Are unpredictable, at times,
I often try to change my mind,
Because I am like a sinking boat
Pulling the sails up a broken mast;

My rhymes no longer float,
My short obituary is signed.

I saw a painting and felt discomfort,
I was confused; I didn't know what to say,
My vivid future was painted gray;
But I realized: that's what the arts are for.

They keep us straight on our toes
And our poetry becomes a prose.

After I lost rosy illusions of my generation,
I seek the truth and climbed the tallest hill,
So far, I found only a single God's creation:
The gap between the healthy and the poor.

The tunes of Blood, Sweat and Tears
Have fallen on our deaf ears.

Trembling Shoulders

You are the one who loves,
Who painlessly can encourage
To leave our frustrations' storage
With iron hands in velvet gloves…

A waterfall of swirling snowflakes
Slowly descends and calmly lands
On your trembling shoulders
Like sparkling shawls or garlands;
No matter what it takes,
You thrill the eyes of all beholders.

I'll become a shadow
Just to follow you,
I'll become a wind
Just to caress you,
I'll become the sun
To warm your heart
And love you.

Unending Journey

I am a worn-out poet,
Even my new ideas ran away,
Death longs for me and shows it,
I crave to see a dawn and then a day.

I ended my so-called unending journey,
But you, my love, are still alive;
The winds of time sway our souls
As if we are a pair of feeble branches
Requesting power of attorney,
Somehow to reenter our abandoned hive.

We navigate between two poles
And hide from life's avalanches...

Venetian Masquerade

They say in Venice:
"No one gets older at the dining table".
They even have three words for one,
Who marries wine and dinner,
A connoisseur, a sybarite, a winner.

Throughout a Venetian masquerade,
I rarely saw attractive faces
Under the weirdest masks and veils;
One windy night, the banners swayed,
My caring fortune filled my sails,
I found love and her embraces.

She was a gorgeous morning light,
She was a golden lining in a cloud;
Our affair enjoyed its primal round,
We loved; it was a really fiery night.

I looked for her in hell and paradise.
God never gifts the same dish twice.

Vodka Tsar

There is no evil,
There is no good.
I didn't choose the bright daylight,
It was a birthright, it was primeval;
I'd rather choose a total darkness,
If the Almighty told me that I could.

Dusks tell the story
Of the days' demise,
Dawns know if the sun will rise,
And bring a glimpse of a fated glory.

My buddies used to lure me to a corner bar,
Where I would outdrink my younger peers;
They called me The Russian Vodka Tsar,
I wolfed my booze and mumbled "cheers".

I've met a dawn that asked me for a dance,
I tango with the nights that made no sense,
I sent to every red sunset my goodbye kiss,
I loved. I never worked a day. I lived in bliss.

I managed to hold my mantle high,
Until it was the time to say bye-bye.

Wisely Masked

She asked:
Whose beds have your boots
Been under?
I didn't crave to feel her sunder;
She knew about me as much
As I wanted to be known,
I have been wisely masked.

Between the fluffy comforters
She played a game of "hard-to-get",
As all the Russians in their fortress
Can't fight but always shout "nyet"!

It's a good time to bury our love
And learn to live without it awhile;
Love grabs you with its iron glove,
And rarely lets you breathe or smile.

I've spoken to my finest thought
That hiked with me along decades,
And realized that love I had,
Was just a sinking boat,
Was only a passing fad,
Just a mirage that quickly fades.

Wedding Carriage

She fell in love with me,
She was my love and muse.
We touched the endless glee,
We trod the isle along the pews.

Life ends in death,
Love is a life that also dies,
Only antipathy survives,
It never takes a final breath.

Our love boat untimely sunk
In the quagmire of marriage.
From time to time, shit visits
Even the best of us…
A loving Venus quickly left
In a cut-rate wedding carriage,
After she dumped our dreams
Under a heartless moving bus.

Our efforts in the pursuit of glee,
Deserve attention of philosophers
Who analyze our love offers,
Besides the genes and pedigree.

Venus Stripped

I didn't count stars
That drowned in the lake,
I calmly watched the ripples.

I never climb a mount
For the saints or devils' sake.

My penny was already flipped,
The Goddess Venus stripped,
I craved her glowing nipples...

We were seduced by beauty of sunrise:
I cherished our glee's incalculable value,
The goddess only knew the price...

I was in paradise, love-smitten
This little poem wasn't written.

Unraveled Quilts

Unraveled quilts reveal a mystery
Of a human carnal knowledge:
I'm not a student of ancient history,
But Adam and Eve for a primal sex
Didn't attend a classy college...
Even today, our growing population
Requires a daily sexual penetration,
A newer name of carnal knowledge.

These theories I learned in college.

Two Sides

Even a modest talent creates its foes,
Only a mediocrity makes only friends;
Although, a guy who's hiking on his toes
Won't reach the fascinating foreign lands.

Some of those friends
Untimely bought the farm,
They didn't use a smoke-alarm
And were decisively unfriended.
They touched the bitter ends
Before their lives have ended.

I twist myself into a pretzel every day,
I try to satisfy my curiosity
That killed the cat.
It's not my stinginess or generosity
That show me the shortest way
To reach a mediocrity I must combat.

Even the thinnest European crepes
Have their two sides;
Even the thickest drapes
Don't hide us from the bloody fights.

Two Hooves

There is another guy in me
Who didn't make it to my birth on time,
I tried to figure out from my pedigree
Whether it was an unexpected glee
Or just a punishment without any crime.

My life rocks on a single ripple:
The more I traveled
And learned about people,
The more I fell in love with pigs.
I lost, I threw a towel,
Went home and locked my digs.

I used to be a hunter,
I shot some ducks and quail,
Hunted deer and wolves.
No more, enough!
Some say, I jumped the bail
And ran on my two hooves
To hug my pigs, my real love.

Town Sleeps

The winds became much stronger,
The forest went into the flames,
The night is lit by fierce bonfire,
The rains can't stop it any longer.

I live in times of heightened stress,
Unfortunately, short of inspirations,
Devoid of good ideas and confused;
This are the times of our separation,
I hate the treatments sharing press,
And throw its advice utterly unused.

My bald head bravely wears a wig,
I simply try to look a little younger,
Some people put a lipstick on a pig,
To camouflage their vicious anger…

Life's going on,
I scoop my ladies
On downtown streets,
Like bay leaves from my soups.
At dusk, when upper town sleeps,
Pimps line up their expensive troops.

Tombstone

In France: Je suis un ami d'une maison,
In Spain: Soy amigo de una casa,
In the US: I am a buddy of a house.

Each one of us may be a second mouse,
The one who always gets the cheese.

I was forgiven begging on my knees,
They carved my name on a marble stone,
Life after death is a kiss-or-miss
I've got the fallen angel as my chaperone.

Life after death is a kiss-or-miss:
One day, we fly above the seven seas,
Another day, we have to visit the abyss.

The Shade

The fear of violence
Is not a place to meet the gods,
It's not a place to find commonsense;
Nobody flies between the lightning rods.

A bird in the hand
Worth two in the bush;
A loud, tone-deaf marching band
Is healthier than a cultural ambush.

We used to call them birds of a feather,
These days they are the birds of prey;
You see their circles in the sky,
Just write your will and say goodbye.

For that I bought a dictionary
And tried to learn to spell.
I am still sipping from that well
And slowly writing my obituary.

Meanwhile, my passing is delayed,
The benches in the sun were taken,
I am quietly waiting in the shade…
The happy end is trying to break in.

Still Soar

What's going on above?
The same as it is below.
I wonder if there is love
Or there is a life to throw.

I borrow wisdom from my doubts
i can't be shy and introverted,
I am a window into a life converted
Into a banner for the hungry crowds.

My intellect distills
The waterfall of thoughts
That used to turn the wheels,
Today, they disconnect the dots.

Nobody cares about what I knew,
Unless they know that a care
About the chosen few,
About those who fought in war
During the horrid days and nights,
My memories of them still soar
Into the new war's shattered sights.

Singing Swan

I was presented to the public
With a few metaphors and epithets;
It was as pleasing as a morning breeze;
I didn't have to pull a rabbit for this trick,
They loved me more than their own pets
I swayed just like a gymnast on a trapeze.

I am totally devoted and unmasked;
But someone in the room abruptly asked
To hold my horses and to hold my breath…
I didn't let him see the dance of death.
I didn't have to jump through hoops
To prove that I am still alive;
I didn't let him hear my oops,
I have a pulse, I even walk and drive.

Back home, in my low-priced motel,
I couldn't sleep but didn't ring the bell,
I only pressed my eyes against a window
To see who makes those nasty noises,
I didn't want to stay in an uncertain limbo,
I longed for much more risks and choices,

Revolutions

I've read the Marxist's manifesto cries:
"Workers of the world, unite!
You'll lose nothing but your chains!
You have a world to win!"
It is a bunch of futile promises and lies:
The terror brought the endless night,
The workers pulled the bloody reins,
And disregarded every known sin...

Poverty leads to revolutions,
The revolutions lead to poverty...
I haven't found yet any solutions,
I crossed all known to me T's,
But didn't place a single dot,
I didn't slash the Gordian knot.

Predicted

My seven unforgiven mortal sins
Have an ability to reinforce each other,
And merge into a torrential desire
To imitate my father:
Get drunk, have sex, and show
That both of us already know
How the human life begins
Before it drowns in a quagmire
Of our daily middleclass routines.

I tried but couldn't stop the fountain
Of my linguistic diarrhea,
I realized, it's not a feasible idea,
The verses pour out of my mind,
They left my wives and friends behind.

I milk my muse and write my verses,
As if it is the Second Coming
After the run of four Apocalyptic horses.
And as in the Book of Revelation,
Predicted and unavoidably forthcoming.

Planet Earth

I was too young,
I was a harnessed trotter,
My song wasn't yet sung,
I only treaded water.

I didn't win a single race,
I've dreamt about fame
But didn't touch its face;
I genuinely liked sunsets,
At dusk, I rolled the dice
And placed my wishy bets.

Today, I hear the truth
Today, I am in the know,
Today, I listen to my youth
I have a seat in the first row.

Enlightenment of our world
Requires a quiet wrath
Of those who walk the path
Toward the buried primal word,
Who float on rising tide of mirth,
Who try to save the planet Earth.

Orchids

I love my temperamental orchids
Quietly bathing in the sun,
They looked like perky lovely brides
Passionately followed by the kids
Carrying the wedding dresses' trains
Thru those ritualistic walks and rides.

Only a few foresaw inevitable pains.

Only wise men unplug themselves
From cute theatrics of the fairy tale,
And contemplate what's written
In the early books on dusty shelves:
All marriages are gently moving trains
That may regrettably derail.

Reality is like a final coffin nail,
Unmasked, no camouflage, no veil.

Nocturnal Cat

I live without lights,
I am a nocturnal cat,
I am a lynx, a real ocelot,
And I am dating in the nights;

From time to time
I even tight the knot...

The daylights lead to my divorces,
Love doesn't let me hold my horses,
They run and set me free
To sail across the innocence of glee.

Life used to slap me silly,
While our street was paved with gold;
No more, it is a long way to Piccadilly,
I learned to see. I pawned my blindfold.

Never Soar

I muttered a few times:
"Those who were born in cages,
Will shred these romantic pages,
They probably will drop their chains,
But someone else will pull the reigns
As our punishment without our crimes.

The rust of this despicable oppression
Eats through our silver-plated hearts,
We don't revolt, we pile the broken parts
As if we signed a pact of nonaggression.

I've been a total stranger
In every soiled and corrupted century
That mercilessly and violently passed,
I was arrested as a wingless fallen angel,
They sent me for eternity in a penitentiary,
Because I told them a harsh truth, at last,
About peace and war,
About hate and love,
About imaginary gods and saints above,
About our lacking souls that never soar.

My Word

"A man is happy if he wants someone,
A happy woman is the wanted one."
That's what a maven Nietzsche wrote
So virginally, bluntly and naively;
For me this whole idea doesn't float
Without any reservations. Really.

I ask you, take my word:
I bet only on Wisdom, Time and Space.
Three cornerstones of our world:
Time is a space for early leavers,
A few on the dot, beside latecomers.
Space is a constant waterfall of time.
These days, civility is definitely dead:
A beast becomes a man,
A manly Nietzsche turns beastly mad,
Completely bare and rather dumb,
Futile and loud like an empty drum.

Time is a mountain I failed to climb,
While Wisdom rises to the Peter's Dome,
No one will touch or have it anymore,
Long live the infinite stupidity galore!

Amazing Void

The crafty preachers bless the wars,
Confessions and remorse
Lead sinners to the gates of bliss,
While righteous march to the abyss.

At times, it's our suffering,
More often, it's our glee,
Become the measures of reality
For those with pearls or a nose ring,
Our faith dissolves in tears of pain;
We joyfully live in this amazing void;
We didn't lose what we couldn't gain.

Ancient Dance

I am right in the midst
Of a nostalgic journey
Into a mystery of Holy Eucharist,
I am consecrating wine and bread,
Devouring The Last and final supper,
Before a resurrection of a single dead,
Who wasted just a day in the abyss's gutter.

I am still visiting that sight…
I am still trying to understand
Why only the Prince of Light
Received a sacred second chance
To lead the human marching band
To a new music for the ancient dance.

Anesthetics

My heavy drinking is anesthetics
That let me write and tolerate
The chronic pains of life…
In spite of my refined aesthetics,
Wellbeing is a constant bloody strife.

I stored a lot of verses in my mind,
I wrote some new, the oldies rested;
Besides, I dated, dined and wined
In bistros where all poets nested.

The swirling, bubbling streams
Of my well-rhymed four liners,
Dug into the hopes and dreams
Like the most fretful coal miners.

I laughed when I was poor and young,
These days, I lost those naughty skills;
Life bared her poisoned riven tongue,
I can no longer drink and pay my bills.

My life turned out to be stinging nettle,
I won't lay down arms and leave,
I bought the biggest kettle
To boil and let go grief.

Asking Price

Life spreads the wings of nights
And undermines the fragile lights
Of my mischievous daydream,
And it defiantly floats downstream.

Only a river of our noisy cars
Competes with the nightly stars.

The well-lit windows of downtown
Fight the melancholy night,
And stitched into a vibrant quilt;
The sun yet didn't drown
And flaunts its red-faced light
As a display of nonexistent guilt.

After I visited my favorite barstool,
I climbed the runway to paradise,
I was clear-eyed- I pilled the wool,
Then hit the sack…
My pillow didn't have a cooler side,
I pulled my good olé silver flask;
For that I didn't need a guide,
I knew the asking price.

Basic Math

No one can stop the rite of spring,
Neither a puppet nor a king.
Society is like a basic math:
If we are equal to the same,
We are equal to each other;
There is a bumpy narrow path
From being lame to a shiny fame,
But if you don't want, don't bother.

Freedom of minds and choices
Allows us to raise our voices,
And being almost totally congruent
To see who's dumb and who is fluent.

Beaming Yolk

Compassion manifests itself
In a disappointment
With a prevailing view
Of the society's enjoyment.

Meanwhile, I navigate Fifth Avenue,
The best of what New York supplies,
A true temptation in disguise,
Under the blazing sun
Which looks just like a beaming yolk,
The clouds are innocently white,
They outfit the sun as a white cloak…

And yet, I am thinking of the moon,
Why still prefer a cold reflected light,
That cast much longer shadows,
The longer memories of me
After I saw my last sunset…

But it is not the final night,
It is not even an evening yet.

Beaten Paths

No matter how hard we hit the gym,
We hardly exercise our lazy brains;
Whether we ride the bikes or trains,
We're only getting muscular and slim.

I pealed embroidery off the olden stories
Instead of playing balls and strikes,
I've got intelligence and worries,
The sea of wisdom crushed the dykes.

I eat and drink a lot, and smoke,
I rarely go outside or use a fan,
I think I am a little bit addicted;
You are predestined to the can,
My friends and foes predicted.

We wind up where it is written
In the good ole' Book of fates;
Those paths are rather beaten,
By all the modest or the greats.

A quiet, self-effacing humble,
A pompous, arrogant highbrow…
They will inevitably tumble.
God knows when, I know how.

Blindfolded Truth

I am not a boat without oars and sails,
I am not a train that chugs along the rails,
I am a want-to-know snooping boy,
Hiding under the pillow his tooth fairy;

Years passed; I run across a vast periphery
Of our nave creator's all forgiving ploy.

I lived in a glossy tower of lies,
I've read a never written verse,
I threw a never thrown dice,
I slept with the church's whores…

These games of my uneasy youth
In the pursuit of a vaguely known bliss
Were noticed by the blindfolded Truth,
Who said: "Don't even aim, you'll miss".

Life is a tragic comedy of ancient Greece:
We fight the wars, neglect a fragile peace,
But then the just and rigit Truth descends,
And none of us will reach the happy ends.

Blue Moon

Once in a blue moon
I crassly faced the crowds
Just outside of my arrogant cocoon
Under the nom de plume
And a wet blanket of dark doubts.

I acted as a Spiderman
And cracked into a building…
A red-faced devastating shame
Required a new masterplan,
Perhaps some polishing and gilding.
My vanity has been kidnapped
To feed the beast,
But not my intellect and soul,
The sun still rises in the East.

I built a quiet house
In someone's trusting heart,
I still continuously browse
At love as the greatest work of art.

Chancing

We crawl to see the shrink controlling our abnormalities,
He is a rearview mirror that parts illusions from realities,
He parts nightmares from blamelessness of our dualities,
Or better yet, he keeps apart our bipolar personalities...

Only a joy of seeing the promised, but evasive paradise
Matches the cheery sunrays dancing on the melting ice,
And equals the unnerving chancing of the rolling dice...

Life is a gambling ship that doesn't sink if you pay the price.
Childlike Man

Only a mindless or a childlike man
Could have conceived or planned
A life what it became.
Predictably, shit hit the fan,
Because the rest of us didn't exist
Or were ignored or banned.
While we have found whom to blame,
The risen sun is giggling in the East.

I had a heavy and uneasy life,
And after all is said and done,
I must admit, I'd bring a knife
While my opponents got a gun.

My wheel of life once started,
Didn't yet stop to rest in peace,
I am not yet brokenhearted,
I long for the Golden Fleece.

I walk the wire stretched over the abyss,
My lifespan is a constant hit-or-miss.

Childlike Man

Only a mindless or a childlike man
Could have conceived or planned
A life what it became.
Predictably, shit hit the fan,
Because the rest of us didn't exist
Or were ignored or banned.
While we have found whom to blame,
The risen sun is giggling in the East.

I had a heavy and uneasy life,
And after all is said and done,
I must admit, I'd bring a knife
While my opponents got a gun.

My wheel of life once started,
Didn't yet stop to rest in peace,
I am not yet brokenhearted,
I long for the Golden Fleece.

I walk the wire stretched over the abyss,
My lifespan is a constant hit-or-miss.

Chosen Aim

My sybaritic life is obvious to all,
The pleasures are my chosen aim;
In the pursuit of self-indulgence
I asked the gods at the Wailing Wall
To let me live my life and I will claim
The crown of epicurean abundance.

The gods pledged to return
And spend more time with me,
But wished for me to learn
Not only tough and rough, but filigree.

Before I learned to write,
I learned to live,
I learned to love,
I learned to fight;
When that was not enough,
I learned to laugh,
And only then I learned to cry
Under the blanket of the night.

And then it was too late
To resurrect my dreams and hopes,
They were hung out at the heaven's gate,
My angels asked to bring not filigree
But tough and rough, long-lasting ropes.

Come True

Some questions never die,
Some answers never live.
It's all in the eye
Of the beholder;
This theory is even older
Than the initial sin of Eve.

Our shadows always follow us,
They know every minus, every plus,
They know every lie and every truth,
They still remember our youth.

The diamonds of morning dew
Slept under the blanket of the night,
The tree of knowledge slowly grew,
As a safe haven for our minds delight.

There are some better days ahead
With gleams of come true wishes;
Besides my cold and unkempt bed,
My dusty rooms and dirty dishes.

Competition

As always there are good and evil
Between our planet's poles.
When there are only two compete,
The situation changes fast,
They often trade their roles
There can be just a single winner,
The second place is a dead last.

They march to their own beat.

If one is ready to succumb or faint,
He turns into a sinner,
The other morphs into a saint;
A so-called fallen angel disappears,
The instant winner is a real danger.
He poisons with anxiety my peers.

Constant Dread

Six somber-faced pallbearers
Carry a heavy body of a dead,
As every one of our planet's dwellers,
He had some valid views and errors;
As each of us he hid a constant dread.

The single greatest source
Of our satisfying daily pleasures
Is imitation of the talented, of course;
We feel as if we own their treasures.

The talented gift us with everything,
But most of us have almost nothing
To share, to give away or to disperse,
No one will benefit from our tiny purse.

I guess, I have some talents,
I noticed, people plagiarize
Some of my rather wasted lines
That I had planned to resurrect;
They satisfied their greedy eyes,
But missed some warning signs:
Eat, drink but don't be wrecked…

In French, I say je suis un peu timide,
But I if you use me, place a hefty bid.

Cutting Edge

I put aside hardboiled eggs,
It was too late for breakfast,
Too early to enjoy my lunch;
I couldn't even think of food,
I liked her lengthy legs,
I definitely liked all the rest.
I made a wish and knocked on wood.

I had my coffee with a biscuit
As a reminder of my pledge
To cook tonight grilled brisket
And stay alive on a cutting edge.

I like to iron the unending threads
Of stitched with the lines highways;
I'm so fast; the others turn their heads,
There's no time to hate or to embrace.

Even the famous cocaine user Holmes
Studied a magnitude of broken condoms;
Poor children without love and hugs,
So-call unwanted kids' unsmiling mugs
Become grim faces of the most wanted.

Farewell, I have to run,
The bells already toll for me,
I am the hounded one,
I have to flee.

Dancing Candlelight

I never tried to cease
My foggy and a shortsighted vision,
I made a half-baked decision,
Which burned the ancient bridge,
I used to cross some time before,
Searching for a lasting peace,
Somewhere beyond the nasty war.

There are two sides to a pancake,
No matter how thin you make it.
Just flip to see the other side,
And don't expect your moral guide
To tell the truth; he'll fake it.

I failed to clear with morning dew
And with a morning breeze
My convoluted and outdated view,
I lost the fight and wasted peace.

Tealeaves foresaw this day,
Sunsets foresaw this night,
Our fates lie on a silver tray
Lit by a dancing candlelight.

Deaf Stranger

When God gifts us enormous intellects
He borders them with bleeding hearts;
Only the brainless get God's respects
Without science, visual and literary arts.

We infinitely cherish people's kindness,
But memorize their hatred even longer;
Only a meek, lackluster nothingness
Despised by most of us much stronger.

A deep experience is a cute way
To call our failures and mistakes;
All those who flaunt their past
Don't have a life of glee today.
I'll do my best or what it takes
To live or rest in peace, at last.

When I get older and lose my sight,
I will be able to visualize much more.

One day, I'll send a slow-moving angel
To bring my rather never wanted death.
Meanwhile, I'll befriend a total stranger,
Preferably careless, numb, and deaf,
Who'll never hear my parting breath.

Drift Away

The lonely quiet avenues
Don't like the noisy streets,
Even the seven rainbow hues
Don't only for the front row seats.

Our fear of silence lived forever,
The noises never disappear,
In vain, we pull the lever,
To try to stop our planet's sphere.

It has been written in the sky
Above our Earth,
But later blown away.
I never figured out why
We permanently drift away
From birth
Until the final day.

My crystal ball is clouded forever,
I can't foresee sunrises and sunsets,
I can't predict my new endeavor,
The game is over, no more bets.

Ego Wins

The red-faced sun
Hopelessly dove
Into his own sunset.
A show-life must go on,
Today, it's Genghis Khan,
Tomorrow, it's Napoleon.

My life is more-less
Evenly divided
Between the busy nights
And lazy days:
I work, I never sleep at night,
Though, it's a bit one-sided,
Next day, I rectify my stress.

We are forever well-connected
By our seven mortal sins,
Thus, everyone is unexpected
To lose. At least, his ego wins.

We generally agree,
Yet, argue in a semantic battle,
The walls and windows rattle,
Our pride won't let us stop or flee.

I left the maze of this ill-fated view,
I meander through a quiet avenue.

Entirely Free

The endless lullabies of rain
Caress my wounds and pain,
My slowly healing scars
Under the glimpse of dawn,
Under the freezing worn-out sun,
Under the scorching nightly stars.

I thank you Lord for not loving me,
I am so happy to be entirely free
In my front row comfortable seat;
Although, the globe still moves
Under my exhausted feet;
I only plod them like the hooves.

I reached a "tipping point",
I walk a razor of a ridge;
It is a good time to roll a joint
Before I cross the burning bridge.

Existential Despair

I checked the hand I have been dealt,
I had no chance, I dropped the ball,
I knew the rules: winners take all,
The losers fill the empty caskets.
No matter what I knew or felt,
My peers were happy picnic baskets.

I am in the state of existential despair,
I'm fearful of what still lies ahead,
Not that the world is fair or totally unfair,
Not that the world stands on its head,
But that we slide into banal and tedious,
Or toward dreadful and hideous.

Even the gods can't stop the slide…
Meanwhile, the world enjoys the ride.

No one can hold our world together,
It looks like a broken chain,
And we, the birds of a feather
March on the dead-end lane.

Fainted Light

I drank my Bordeaux wine
With a few cubes of ice,
It was damn rude and vicious,
But rather utterly delicious.

I am drinking like an alcoholic,
Who needs a doctor or a nurse,
Nobody gives a dime
For what I do or say,
But I am an actor in this play,
I tailor just a little bit of time
And write another, better verse…

My turbulent relation
With Mexican Tequila
Has ended in divorce;
She's got some cash
And a huge taxation,
I've got a Seaside villa.

A hut or a chic ballroom,
I can't sojourn my gloom,
I am forever melancholic,
Surrealistic and symbolic,
Unless I die and fly away
Into the dreamland's night,
Into eternity of fainted light
The realm of inert and gray.

Falling Snowflakes

The falling snowflakes,
Seem innocently pure,
They are the unforgiven souls.
The judge of heavens hit the brakes
And our delicate divinity of goodness
Morphed into out-of-date manure…
The rivers, oceans, seas, and lakes
Bleached the Dead Sea scrolls
Then hid them in the times' potholes.

We act without stages and new roles.

All of a sudden, my angel reappeared,
It only brought exactly what I feared,
The saints won't let me save my grace.
Young angel placed a toothless smile
On his obnoxious badly pimpled face.

That's life. I had to walk my extra mile.

Fated Roles

We are surrounded with greedy beasts
That scar our minds and souls,
And yet, the cunning priests
And honorable thieves,
Besides the other social achievers
Won't let us play the fated roles,
But push us through their sieves,
To morph us from hounds to retrievers.

Is this a chaos or a paradigm?
The predators are fed,
The preys didn't survive.
Our asses dropped the lead,
We crawl and walk, we run and drive,
Our planet Earth is turning on the dime.

Few Thoughts

Life quickly runs;
It is a sprint,
But not a marathon.
Only the lucky ones
May get a hint,
There is no time to yawn.

I trapped a deer in my highlights,
He posed just like a movie star.
I guess we both enjoyed the night,
Each had his own glee,
One was completely free,
Another locked up in his car.

A thief is not who steals,
It is the one who's captured.
As long as one walks on high heels,
His shiny bio will be manufactured.

I reached the bottom,
Yet didn't break my neck
While falling from a basement.
Life is a chilly, rainy autumn,
I am a total wreck,
But crawl out of my effacement.

Film Noir

I built a bar like in the Western films,
My basement turned into a drinking nook,
I flaunt my overvalued cowboy whims,
A shiny counter reflects my trashy look

My life is like a film noir,
I am a supporting actor,
I have a secondary role,
I am not a major star.
I put my shoulder to the wheel
To earn my daily bread and meal.

I seldom see the sky between the twigs,
I seldom feel the gentle morning breeze.
I play in sequences of endless plots,
I only change my pseudonyms and wigs,
Then chat and even wet my eyes.
There's no time to cross the T's,
There is no time to hang the dots
Above the solitary I's.

I want to disappear
Into my lukewarm drink,
Then fall into my chilly bed
Where no one shouts bottoms up;
The helpless human sheep are saved,
The always hungry predators are fed,
I am heading for the final roundup,
The road to bliss is freshly paved.

Final Whistle

Death is a game
Nobody wants to win;
We play the game from thick to thin
Until the final whistle. Who is to blame?

Arrival of the baby-bringing storks
Make clear to me the innocence of truth,
And only then, my loneliness invokes
The tender and magnetic images of youth.

The raindrops fall as if somebody cries,
I watch the Lord-created windy skies,
They range from violent
To chillingly, but nervously disquiet,
They often morph from thunderous to silent.

I still believe that evil is hypnotically seductive,
Deliciously unnerving and thrillingly deviant.
I trust that good is not aggressively proactive,
Good, fortunately, is just a sleepy, quiet giant.

Life is a must-visit movie theatre
That shows just a single picture.
Some came to watch that film,
Some are still watching,
Some have already gone…
They've seen the happy end,
They watch the new life's dawn.

Forbidden Fruits

My wrinkled and saw-it-all face
Reflects the endless joy of victories
Against the daily trivial pursuits;
My life devours years and hours,
Fights tooth and nail, and uses elbows,
And even eats the most forbidden fruits.
Today, I planted new sunflowers,
Because I plan to see tomorrows.

I traveled through the world,
Here is my word:
I met the baby-faced assassins,
They didn't care about their own skins,
They pull the triggers before they aim,
No sympathy, and no remorse or shame.

For them life is a barrel
For shooting fish;
I didn't sing for them a carol,
But death and hell was my firm wish.

I didn't have to jump through hoops,
To prove that I am a decent man,
No one has heard my "oops".
Meanwhile, a better day began.

Freezing Kiss

A life ends only once
In a blue moon,
But when she comes,
We sing the same ole' tune
"Amazing Grace"…
In any case,
Life surely takes its toll,
I've been betrayed
By my resilience,
I cast no shadow on the wall
As if I am a saint forever sinless.

I don't believe in bliss,
I don't believe in the abyss,
That's why death didn't gift me yet
Her final freezing kiss, I bet.

Gloom

Life strolls across eternal nights
Into finality of days,
Passing the convoluted prose of faith
And poetry of our endeavors' lathe…

My mind is questing
Infinity's enchanting end,
While my worn-out body wasting
The hourglasses' priceless sand.

I have no other shoe to drop,
I hit the bottom of my gloom,
And called some neighbors to a table
With hope to trawl a teasing fable
About those who are on top
Or who are resting under in the tomb.

The guests were faceless,
The dinner was as tasteless
As a tissue paper,
Dreary and long as an old skyscraper.

A man is only a summary of deeds,
But not his rosy, sparkling thoughts.
Glimmers of hope are just the weeds
That rise on the abandoned parking lots.

Gloomy Downfall

I have a ripened melon on my shoulders,
I tread the water before I do a cannonball,
I probably bite more than I can chew and ask:
Is this the world you, mighty Zeus, anticipated,
Besides the silliness of the Sisyphus' boulders?

The modern slayers don't need a mask:
A heartless bunch of boisterous teens
Quite ready to be ivy-educated
While escort our coffins to the grave...
Inevitable and gloomy downfall
Of us, of rather shadowy has-beens,
Of a so-called generation of the brave.

Eternal oblivion is self-preservation
Of our collective fragile mind.
We just forget our scars, and pain,
And like in that famous film
We are still dancing in the rain,
Leaving all tragically obvious behind
To build a healthier and, better nation.

Glowing Place

I am looking at a pompous portrait
Of a great poet who is still alive,
And learn to write my stanzas and survive,
But not how to climb, reach fame and thrive.

I didn't write the sacred word
That started our lives,
I am not the greatest poet of the world,
I didn't earn that sparkly rank,
I didn't carve a line that broke the bank,
But I am well known in the drinking dives.

And I'm sure, the literary critics have to face
Rigorous standards of my beloved verses
And tedious mastery of my faultless rhymes
That found their glowing place
In my sophisticated readers' minds and souls
Before the four apocalyptic horses
Bring punishments for some illusive crimes
To our energetic wishes, hopes, and goals.

God Grins

There's no free lunch,
Just tell me how much.

Life is for some to throw,
Life is for me to keep;
Life is for the sun to glow,
Life is for the moon to weep.

The old and murky skies
Don't speak on my behalf;
It's rain; a heavy cloud cries;
While I still sin and laugh.

A gentle stream of hope
Became a mighty waterfall;
Nevertheless,
The chosen fly, the others crawl,
The angels sealed my envelope.

God grins and lets me guess.

Golden Idols

I heard:
The jurors lost their final strife
And I was sentenced to a jolly life,
The longest straw has been drawn,
My future was exciting but unknown.

I knew:
Don't ever touch the golden idols,
You'll need to wash your hands.
We live among the vicious rivals,
And no one knows where each stands.

I sang:
The sun rolled into the noon,
The shadows stretched much longer,
I waited, wished to see you soon,
It only made my thirst much stronger.

Quite soon we took the deepest breath,
And froze our tumultuous relation;
We felt as if it was a sudden death
And our bodies longed for a cremation.

But lives went on,
None of us died,
The French say "c'est si bon":
She found a great groom,
I found a great bride…
No one is flying on the broom.

These days, we are good friends,
The means were crowned by the ends.

Has Gone

The flow of a faucet
Is not the flow of a drain,
We taste our love and toss it,
Then taste again, in vain.

Wine lost its taste,
My daily bread is dry.
Long live, insufferable waste
Under the never smiling sky.

I guess, I've had enough,
I knew a lifelong love
I have arrived. Go I must
As dust to dust.

My flesh is buried in a battlefield,
Not in a boneyard of a church.
My lips are permanently sealed,
I hinted no to the heroes search.

My wondering has gone,
The skies and I are one.

He Winked

My life has been a thousand missteps,
I crossed too many lines,
I didn't pay attention to the hedges,
I've seen forgiven and forgotten debts,
Meanwhile I carved my humble lines,
And didn't waste my empty pledges.

It wasn't just a pocket change,
It was my all-hands-on-deck life,
It was a brutal, noisy shooting range
From eight to five
Before the sleepless nights,
And then, again the futile fights.

I was the devil's advocate,
As long as he is free,
I'd get my cut
And hid his shady pedigree
Of a noncompliant Lucifer,
Who used to be the brightest angel,
But fell and missed the sweet affair,
The star of Bethlehem and Jesus' manger.

I rest in peace today,
And travel through the Milky Way
Among the sinless and the winged.

Last night, I saw the Lord. He winked.

Heavy Pestle

I write, therefore I am alive,
I grind and mix my words with a heavy pestle
In a deep mortar of my romantic strive,
Maybe in vain, I tirelessly, continually wrestle
With inner demons of my poetic life
From five to eight and then from eight to five,

Life is a comedy of horrors
And daily reaps our applauds
Death is a tragedy of dated jokes
That puts us in a lethargic sleep,
In spite of my horrendous odds,
My worries are skin-deep,
I dropped these autocratic yokes.

I treasure every facet of my troubled life,
Yet, I am not pure as Caesar's wife,
But I am happy as a picnic basket,
And sad as if I shoulder my own casket

Homage to Pablo Neruda

If you don't hear the judge's gavel,
If you don't feel the pulse of life,
If you don't know passion,
If you don't read and travel,
If you don't have a dream,
You lost your strife,
You lost your self-esteem,
And it's too late for a confession.

You started to pay for self-denying,
You started your lethargic dying…

Horoscope

I have received from the above
My all-I-have-to-know horoscope:
I didn't learn about love,
I didn't learn about hope,
I didn't learn about blinding lights,
I didn't learn about sleepless night,
I didn't learn from being here before,
I simply left my shadow on the floor.

Humble Bard

I shanked my ball into the woods,
Just to avoid my gloomy moods;
Sometimes, I reconnect my wires
Just to revive my sweet desires.

Some say: "my verse is a waste of time,
And I don't have a time for fun and love".
They never have enough,
They need to make a deal or borrow…
Meanwhile, I love to carve my rhyme,
I live in glee, they stroke their sorrow.

Our world's changing of the guard,
Means nil; I am your humble bard;
I write my poetry and sing my songs
For you, to whom it all belongs.

Impenetrable Wall

This way or another, but we get paid:
For trusting someone we are betrayed,
For self- confdence we are ridiculed,
Named arrogant and even schooled.

I need to have a little bit of grit,
I drown in a never-ending louche;
In any case, I reached my end of wit
And acted as a bad-tempered grouch.
My ex flaunts fashions on a runway,
While I am sleeping on a scruffy couch
With masochistic pleasures of dismay.

I lived through happy days,
I tasted some bitter fruits of life,
I strolled between my gains and losses,
My truck devoured dozens of highways,
In vain, I tried to catch a falling knife,
I even argued with my heartless bosses.

I've seen and done it all:
At times, I acted as a coward or a hero,
A life experience is just a rearview mirror,
But I have learned to wait;
I am still looking for the sacred gate
In bliss' impenetrable wall.

Incoherent Dots

There can be only one best,
Just take my word and bank it,
But there is another side
In every blanket
Created for all the rest,
Who had to choose the downside.

The bells will ring
When there is nothing else to lose,
When there is nothing more to gain.
My freedom is the rite of spring,
It is my trusted loyal muse,
A life without even a golden chain.

My freedom is a flight into the space
Away from the baffling Gordian knots,
Away from the constant vicious race,
Away from the pile of incoherent dots.

Infamous Apple

The same infamous apple
From the tree of knowledge
In which Eve sunk her teeth
Fell on Isaac Newton's head.
The apples fall under the trees;
It means Sir Isaac spent
A day or two in Eden;
I've been there twice,
Take my encouraging advice:
The pretty place is not forbidden,
It even cures our curiosity disease.

Although, I'm relatively smart,
My intellect like yeast, still rises,
I'm not immune to most surprises.
I went to church and read the sign:
"Turn off the light,
And you will see the miracles
Of darkness."
I closed my eyes and saw that sight,
There were two hugging vehicles,
Two loving and inseparable partners.

I must admit,
Whether the sights are dark or lit,
I realize, our life is going on,
And in the wake of my surprise,
I hope to witness yet another dawn.

Long Distance

Life cruelly passes by,
I watch it with discretion,
And share my kindness
With the frugal ration
Until I wave my last goodbye.

I walk the avenues
Between the squares
Of my existence,
Along the stripes and stars,
Under the circles
Of the moon and sun,
Surrounded with ugly news.
Life seems like a long distance
With wars and peace,
With wounds and scars,
With hope to see another dawn.

Each spring with some theatrics,
The world becomes a little newer;
I pull another rabbit for the tricks,
But bit-by-bit my age devours me;
Long live my sparkling daily glee!

Manners

Death telegraphed her thoughts
And lifted all the boats;
My life displayed good manners:
I watched the gloomy tide of grief
Embraced half-risen banners.

A snifter of a warmed up brandy
Brought sentimental fragments
Of my nostalgic melancholy:
I miss reality; not something trendy
Like fashionable kitschy garments
Of those who yelp about someone Holy.

I have no showy stile,
But inborn elegance
Which is a solid magnet
That pulls all metal parts
Of people toward me.

Long live life's gentility and filigree!!!

Misty Caves

I can no longer shoot fish in the barrels,
I have no will to sing the Christmas carols.

I am on my awe-inspired willful descent
Into the deepest, no-way-out misty caves,
Where our fates were painfully bent,
Where yellow cowards lead the braves.

I couldn't chase that destination,
I only morphed my lies into the truths,
I even heard the end of my unwritten song,
I sensed that everything went awfully wrong,
I had no goal, no purpose, and no aspiration,
But only the unworthy issues of our youths…

I am walking on the raiser's edge,
I am turning on the dime,
There is no time
For my confession or a candid pledge…

Moving Target

Love is a moving prey,
Even the cupids' darts
Miss our thirsty hearts
Day after day…

Love is a hand- knotted carpet,
Love is a glamorous affair
Love is a moving target,
That needs a constant care…

My heart is like a running motor,
Call me a loving culprit,
Call me a loving villain;
Even a romantic weeping willow
Must bend to love the water
The way it seems to fit.

My Barge

I'd rather suffer in a feisty New York City
Then dwell in a quiet village that is friendly,
I'd rather be an object of jealousy and envy,
Then harvest from my pals sympathy and pity.

I live alone,
But I am still in charge;
I didn't abdicate my throne,
I am still a captain of my barge.

My cellphone prefers a total silence,
Although, the old alarm clock rings,
Life treats me with a veiled violence,
I hear the fat and vicious lady sings.

Even under a peacock's tail
Hides an ordinary chicken ass,
Even an extraordinary crystal
Is cut but still a leaded glass.

Sooner or later
Wisdom affects my mind,
It is my presumed creator
Gifts vision even to the blind.

I have arrived
At eighty six,
My soul and intellect survived
Life's devastating bag of tricks.

My Dimes

I couldn't live in a cocoon,
I had to know what, when and why,
I was reacting and reasonably soon
Would try to break the dead-end tie…

I earned the calluses on both my hands,
I poked the bear and even fought at times,
I've seen the happy ends,
I've seen some heavy losses of my dimes.

I moved from a zone defense
Into a brutal man-on-man offense;
There are no draws in the fray,
There are the predators and prey.

I spent ten years in jail
And learned to spiritedly curse,
To sing just like a nightingale,
To write my enthusiastic verse.
I saw the sky through metal bars,
And pledged, after they set me free,
To do my very best and reach the stars.

My God

My love was ill,
I prayed and asked my God:
"Don't let her die,
I do insist".
As always, He was fully deaf
Or absolutely didn't care,
Or, as many say, didn't exist.

I paid the bill and dumped my soul,
My conscience was already frozen;
So many were called, but very few
Entirely by them, were chosen.

Life is a stage of badness,
Small actors get big roles.
I wear a masterpiece,
A mask of happiness and sadness,
Two masks in one.
The years of wars,
The days of peace.

With no regrets, I emptied
A heavy bag of my desires,
I must admit, I am tempted
To kick my future's tires.

Nostalgic Pains

Some troubling memories
Of my uncomfortable past
Arrived with the fiftieth birthday;
Nostalgic pains
Stubbornly last,
And like the horses' reins
They've lead me into a melancholy
And toward a hideous depression.

But since I lost my trust
In everything that's holy,
I found an obsession,
I drink and gamble,
I travel and play chess.
I am ecstatic, I confess

Older Broom

I still can't cut my path to greatness
And satisfy my vanity and pride,
Although, as one of the older brooms
I am familiar with the corners
With hidden fruits of literary carnage,
While silence of my angels deafens.
I cannot bear this any longer...
The wings of Pegasus grow stronger,
Now and then I long for a good ride
Across the innocence of heavens
Through their enormous rooms
Filled with the crying critics-mourners
Missing the fallen Tree of Knowledge.

Others Cry

God said he planned to cede the reigns
Of his disruptive, self-defacing world
To angels and some other flying saints,
But fortunately failed to keep his word.

A fallen, but still an angel, Lucifer
Usurped the yet unknown universes,
And regularly sends his four fatal horses
To finish up that hardly started world.

My eyes are piercing wilderness
In the pursuit of echoes of my despair,
My rather single-minded loneliness,
And my anxiety can no longer bear.

I often laugh,
When all the others cry;
It is my hostile bluff,
It is my scruples say goodbye.

Regrettably

In my pursuit of a happy time
I came across a four-leaved clover;
There is no punishment without crime,
Regrettably, my search is over.

A tender dawn and a fiery sunrise
Took glee, wrapped it and sent
To our bleeding hearts and loud cries;
Regrettably, we lost that kind descent.

Nobody reads the ancient comedies,
We keep them on a dusty shelf,
They turn into the modern tragedies;
Regrettably, the history repeats itself.

Remorseless Sinners

The more I live and learn about people,
The more I love pigs, dogs and horses.
I want to burn my sentimental verses,
To get a drink, not to be slammed,
Then climb my church's steeple,
A little closer to our so-called creator.
As a result I'll be damned,
But he will better hear my heartfelt cry:
"What have you done?
You are the one,
Who satisfied your morbid whims
In almost seven quite capricious days.
Much later you even sacrificed your son,
So harshly killed by your chosen hordes.
I have no justifying words,
That futile death failed to correct us,
He had been pitched under a moving bus;
We are the same remorseless sinners…
I'm not even angered, I'm stunned.
For what you haven't done,
Before too long, you'll be forever shunned."

Revolutions

I've read the Marxist's manifesto cries:
"Workers of the world, unite!
You'll lose nothing but your chains!
You have a world to win!"
It is a bunch of futile promises and lies:
The terror brought the endless night,
The workers pulled the bloody reins,
And disregarded every known sin…

Poverty leads to revolutions,
The revolutions lead to poverty…
I haven't found yet any solutions,
I crossed all known to me T's,
But didn't place a single dot,
I didn't slash the Gordian knot.

Seven

I climb the seven hills
Of the eternal city Rome,
Relaxing in the shadows
Cast by the Peter's Dome
Under the seven colored bows
Flaunting their glory in the sky
Above our planet's seven seas.

The primal truth is out of sight
Behind the seven seals of revelation;
The end of time and our salvation,
Reviling both, depression and delight.

The seven trumpets of the seventh seal
Were blown by two great archangels,
But after that, the seven total strangers
Began to turn the cruel apocalyptic wheel.

So Long

There is no truth without a debate,
Thus if and when you disagree,
Convincingly present your view,
Whether it is provocative and new,
Just pull your horns and wait,
Truth is a jewel, nobody gets it free.

Perhaps, it doesn't matter in a way,
But every night all cats look gray;
The silhouettes of hawks or doves
Against a dark sky, look the same;
In time, even our everlasting loves
Become completely lame...

The sun will always rise,
I wonder, when the sunny ray
May close its eyes and sleep,
Or close its eyes and pray,
Or throw its never lucky dice
And weep.

Meanwhile, I tortured my guitar,
Nobody liked my poetry and song;
I felt just like a hopeless falling star,
But made a heartfelt wish:" So long".

Something New

At times, our life seems weird
Among the fearful and feared.

I never introduced
The element of fear
Into my days even in schools,
Where our cruel teachers used
To dominate
All what we could read or hear,
Although, there were some fools
And fear was certain in their fate.

Among the hunchbacked
We seem stretched in caskets,
Among the gravely wrecked
We're happy as the picnic baskets.

The freshest morning dew
Served a few lovely drinks
For always thirsty clover,
The night is over,
The sky is ready to get lit,
The future slyly winks,
Expecting something new…

Squeaky Floor

Nobody halts wars and rites of springs,
Neither the puppets, nor the kings:
A blade-thin stream of a red-hot light
Streamed on my squeaky floor
As a forewarning of a bloody fight:
Some powerholders declared a war.

We heard the rattling sables
But didn't pay attention;
Nobody left their real passion,
The radiantly lit gambling tables.

I raised the rigging of my boat,
And sailed along the river trough;
It was a bald-faced "coying":
My inborn bravery was off,
I knew where I was going,
I loathe a casket as my overcoat.

Subconscious

I know where my hearty notions dwell,
In chest, slightly below my mind;
Subconscious is my wisdom's well,
It is enormously mysterious inside…

I am correct only two times a day,
Just like the old grandfather clock,
For some it is a quiet time to pray,
I hear tic-toc, tic-toc, tic-toc…

I waste no time for a prayer,
For God my ethics is a player.
I also waste no time for wrath,
I simply give my soul a bath.

Only idealistic grooms and brides
Believe in the cloudless tomorrows,
They trust know-it-all angelic guides,
I trust God won't erase their sorrows.

My Tale

My memory is not a rusty nail
On which I hang my written pages;
It is my uneasy, happy life, it is my tale,
It is my honest portrait painted for the ages.

.

This Hook

I have no other shoes to drop,
I have no other cheeks to turn;
I wouldn't even dream to stop
To see and hear, to think and learn.

I can't tread water any more,
I am ready to get in,
I'll crawl, I'll walk, and I'll run,
I am a true believer.
My problem isn't a mortal sin,
My problem isn't the blazing sun,
My problem is a deteriorating liver.

I walk along the church's nave
To see the images of crucifixion;
I still and probably naively crave
To separate the truth and fiction.

Tightly Locked

I was invited to serve my verses,
They chewed them at the tables;
They clapped with hoofs like horses
Who grind their straw in the stables.

At last, I pulled a rabbit from a hat:
I sang, the audience was shocked
As if I hit them with a baseball bat;
I knew, I reached the door of fame,
Regrettably, the door was locked.

The snobbish critics were appalled
By my, as they said, awkward stile,
Although, my rhymes easily trolled,
I was laconic, I didn't chew the fat:
At times, I cry; sometimes, I smile,
I blend a beer and a great "Moet".

I saw again that door and knocked,
The door of fame was tightly locked.

Treasure Trough

I read a lot and often witness
The uninspired use of language:
The lines are absolutely wingless,
No life, no passion, no outrage
Their verse is not a racing horse,
It's just an extra penny in a purse.

I drown in a downpour of mediocrity,
Yet, tapping onto a treasure trough
Of the ancient Greco-Roman art
That burns my vanity and pride
On the poetic kitchen stove,
And lets the other sins restart.

I found both cornerstones of paradigm,
It's a virtual quintessence of all that is:
Ten even tainted pennies produce a dime,
What's good for ganders is good for geese.

Trusted Thief

My buddy who betrayed me once,
Can be forgiven,
But never loved and hugged
As if he broke my arms.
Though, I'm by a kindness driven,
I am not drunk or drugged.

Again, I need a trusted thief:
Only the truth erases
Deep wrinkles of the eternal grief
From our knowing-it-all faces.

Via Delarosa

Life is a tragedy
For my emotional awareness,
But may become a comedy
Often out of love or fairness.

Chess is a game of memories and minds,
A game of blinders and unexpected finds.
I was quite nervous, at the moment,
But firmly shook the hand of my opponent.

He won, he kicked my fragile mind
Between the eyes with grief.
A day or two, I whined:
Should I respond in kind?
Should I avenge? Should I forgive?

My conscience is a yoke I have to carry,
It is a cross I drag through Via Delarosa.
I'm passionate, my moods may vary…
My predecessors used to say,
Life is not poesy but is a boring prosa.

The fire of strong emotions
Engulfed my realistic intellect.
My hopes forever sunk or wrecked
In the world's seven thirsty oceans.

Warped Mirrors

I never knew the names of angels,
I only tried to recognize their deeds;
Two wings, nevertheless, the strangers,
That chucked their good and evil seeds.

I lived like a starving shark,
I wrote, I hardly ever slept;
I was the only poet on Noah's ark,
They listened to my rhymes and wept.

At times, I tread the murky waters,
Among the bottom feeders,
In the pursuit of dimes and quarters,
Routinely tossed by my devout readers.

My love was a hundred kisses deep,
My life was like a scrumptious wine,
I am ready for my final leap,
I am ready for my final breath.
And then, no one will whine,
No one will weep.

Even the duly noted lives of heroes
Will disappear without a trace;
Only my death will leave her ugly face
In warped and cunning mirrors.

Wasted Chances

I wasted chances
To dive into a river
Of real monies;
I am a hardworking beaver
Who stocks lose branches
And builds the dams
For fish and other dummies.

None of my deeds
Is worthy of a book,
Nevertheless, my book
Is worthy of your reading.
I am still searching in the weeds
And ambiguity is quietly receding.

The truth has to be told:
I wonder why Jesus needs me,
I am not ready for the final flight;
The Chief Creator broke the mold
And set me absolutely free
To eat and drink, to write and fight.

My soul couldn't avoid the rockets,
My death certificate was signed;
What's left of me?
Only my empty pockets
And my aristocratic pedigree,
Never disgusting, always kind.

Autumn

I didn't hit rock-bottom,
No grief, no bitter tears;
It is the golden autumn
Of my enamored years.

The swirling, falling leaves
Of thousands poetic pages
Just like confessing thieves
Quietly whisper to the ages.

Most Wanted

My birth certificate is a multi-headed dragon,
But even a latent life ends on a meat wagon.

The shock of the stimulating new
Or the retrieval of the boring old.
The darkness of a pessimistic bleu
Or the optimistic but a careless gold.

I lived amid the hangers for their uniforms.
They always played without the full decks.
I managed to escape the deadly storms;
I tried to float above the human wrecks.

No one grows older at the dining table,
I take my time and drink after my meals;
Therefore, I am undeniably quite able
To turn my already rusty wheels.

Don't even try to pedal my canoe,
Don't mess with my earned peace.
I still have more than you can chew,
My mug is on the most wanted list.

Simply Tangled

She moved as if she liked to tango.
The rest of women simply tangled.
I said: "Let's tango to the end of love."
She said: "You sound like a hawk,
But I prefer a dove."
I had to take a walk.

I asked the ancient leafless trees,
"Reveal the secrets you so tightly kept."
The maples laughed, the willows wept,
I let their secrets rest in peace.

Between a bowl of water
And the dancing blades of fire,
I am doomed. I will be slaughtered.
Just as an object of someone's desire;
Just like a canary in the mine.
Just like a pearl surrounded by swine.

All dreams are lost
For me and my old peers;
Only our mothers knew the cost
Of sleepless nights and bitter tears.

Nevertheless, my life will never end
Like a nostalgic song.
Like an unwritten verse,
Or music of a passing marching band.
God said:" So long,
I'll see you later in another universe."

Almighty Puppeteer

We never see the roots.
We only watch the surface blooms,
And yet, we march across our dirty boots,
While the unescapable final judgement looms.

The snow melts beneath our feet.
We are still welcomed here,
And our hearts begin to beat
Pulled by the Almighty Puppeteer.

We hold the wrong end of the world equation.
We hold the erratic see-saw of good and evil.
Expecting nothing but a dire upheaval
In our pursuit of the most devious evasion
By those who have to lead and guide
By the corrupted angels of the darker kind.

Our struggle isn't ending.
Those wingless angels never fly,
But crawl and heartlessly demanding:
"Hang them high!"

Gambit

It was my bold and risky gambit.
I lulled my struggle with adversity.
I simply promised to admit
My dirty-old-man perversity.
I still prefer a middle-aged maturity
To a so-called innocence and purity.

Don't let me sleep,
The past is laid to rest.
Some lost, some tried to win.
The future is not cursed or blessed.
My fears and doubts may slip in.

Don't let me sleep,
Or I will miss the Second Coming,
Or I will miss my angel's sacred humming,
Or I will miss the sunsets and sunrises,
Or I will miss the boredom and surprises.

Don't let me sleep,
Or I will miss the lesser of two evils,
Or I will miss the smaller of two fakers,
Or I will miss the kinder of two givers,
Or I will miss my smirking undertakers.

On Bail

If silence is wisdom of a gifted one,
Then it is a safe haven for a fool,
Then it is easier for a midnight sun
To drown in a tiny swimming pool.

Our world is dark and violent;
We manufacture our convoluted tales,
Only the fallen remain silent,
We are the felons who jumped their bails.

A madman is a rehearsal of a dreamer
Who wonders over a hard day's night.
I am not pardoned of all past misdemeanor.
The lifelong tunnel ends. There is no light…

No one suspects stupidity in me.
I am quite open-minded with my friends.
They are familiar with my pedigree,
While I am balancing my odds and ends.
They have a total freedom of imagination.
They read the poems that left my station.

I am living on borrowed time.
I cannot repay my massive debts.
The creditors will catch my rhyme
With their cruel and unforgiving nets.

Behind the Final Curtain

Our winter dreams are mocked.
Our frozen screams are locked.
Good actors imitate; great steal.
The mediocre wait for a free meal.

Victorious Nike spread her wings.
I stood and watched in awe.
I thought it was the rite of springs,
But it was just a short-lived thaw.

A tattered page
Of yet unwritten story
Looks like a golden cage
Hung on the wall of worry.
We are all actors on the stage
Competing for the glory.
Only the end is yet uncertain
Looming behind the final curtain.

Life-stage is loaded with the toys
For those who wouldn't play
In childhood and youth
For those who heard the voice,
For those who knew the way,
For those who knew the truth.

The angels try to choose between
The glory of the champions
And loneliness of actors in defeats.
Our fates foretold but unforeseen
As a result of endless tampering
With our fortunes' balance sheets.

The show must go on
The actors hadn't gone.

Epilogue

My memory is not a rusty nail
To hang my badly written pages,
It is my happy, yet uneasy life. It is my tale,
It is my candid portrait painted for the ages.

Epilogue

With the deepest pain and sadness in my heart, I have to say
The more I learn about people, the more I like the pigs.

Acknowledgements

I am deeply grateful to Judith Broadbent
For her uniquely skilled guidance and generous stewardship
For her unyielding yet wise editing which gives me enough space
To freely exercise my whims.

To a great artist, Mary Anne Capeci, who graciously allowed me
To use her paintings for some of my books.

To Anna Dikalova for her support and sincere belief in my success.

I am profoundly in debt to Dan Canale for his thoroughly detailed
And brilliant analysis and fruitful advices.

To all my friends for their genuine advice and enthusiasm.

Printed in the United States
by Baker & Taylor Publisher Services